English Grammar Workbook for HIGH SCHOOL Grades 9th-12th

Self-Paced Workbook to Improve Grammar and Writing Skills

Cleave Bourbon B.A. M.A.

Shadesilver Publishing

Contents

Introduction and What's New in this UPDATED First Edition

Grammar and the parts of speech are the foundation of effective communication. There is no inflection in text. Sometimes you can't tell if someone is being sarcastic or thoughtful. In order to express such concepts in writing you have to be good at using grammar. Without a solid understanding of the rules and nuances of grammar, it can be difficult to convey your message clearly and effectively. In this book, we'll take an in-depth look at the rules of grammar and the parts of speech, providing you with the tools you need to elevate your writing and communication skills to the next level.

This workbook was written with the high school learner in mind. High school learners should master sentence and paragraph writing before they begin writing essays and long form papers in college. I also included some advanced English Grammar the average high school learner may not be aware of quite yet. These are just introductory, and they should not pose significant difficulty. The more advanced grammar concepts are located in the second part of the workbook.

Happy Learning!

Updated First Edition:

1. **Corrected a few minor mistakes and minor typos.**

2. **Added a missing answer key for the subject and predicate paragraph exercise.**

3. **Added instruction and exercises for simple and complete subjects**

and predicates to chapter 13.

4. **Added answer keys for simple and complete subjects and predicates.**

How to Use this Book

This workbook is designed to be at the higher end of high school learning. If you are here from my middle school version of this workbook, you are going to see some similar exercises and examples from that book. I just made the same sentences more complicated and more suitable for high school readers and learners. I wrote the examples, exercises, and worksheets at a high school reading levels. Grade levels are arbitrary especially with homeschooled children. The rule of thumb is to push learning to the edge of understanding. I encourage you to follow this book in order. Some of the beginning concepts might be easy, but it builds on itself as the learner progresses though the workbook.

This book is organized into two parts. The first chapters cover basic grammar, probably more than you really want to know. Plus, I throw in some tips and tricks I have learned over the years. The second part delves into the more advanced grammar usage. Each chapter has exercises at the end of the section to help with understanding. After the exercises are full worksheets. Complete each section and mark it off on the included progress checker.

Learning and utilizing English grammar is like playing a musical instrument. At first you look at the notes on the staff and coordinate with your hands and fingers where that note is played on the instrument. Eventually, with practice, you no longer think "this is an F sharp and is played this way on the instrument," and instead you see the note on the staff and just automatically go to it and play it. Grammar is the same. Eventually, with practice, you just go there without thinking about it. You place commas where they belong, use the correct noun to match the correct verb and so on. It's really that easy!

Part 1

Parts of Speech and Grammar Usage

Chapter 1

Nouns and Noun Types

Now we can get started on the parts of speech. The next two chapters will explore nouns. They are essential to the structure of a sentence. Being able to identify them is crucial.

Nouns are the foundation of any sentence. In this chapter, we'll explore the different types of nouns, their functions in a sentence, and the rules for using them correctly.

1.0 Definition of Nouns:

A noun is a word that identifies a person, place, thing, or idea (concept). It is often referred to as the naming word of a sentence. In simpler terms, a noun is a word that is used to name something. The subject noun is literally what the sentence is about.

Basic Types of Nouns: common, proper, concrete, abstract, countable, un-countable, collective, and compound.

1.1 Common Nouns:

Common nouns are the most basic type of noun. They are used to name ordinary, everyday objects, people, or places. Examples include cat, bike, and town.

Used in a sentence: Everyone piled into the **car. Car** is a common noun.

1.2 Proper Nouns:

Proper nouns are used to name specific people, places, or things. You can have a shoe (common) but when you name that shoe (Nike) it becomes proper. Proper nouns always begin with a capital letter. Examples include Kimberly, Los Angeles, and Pepsi-Cola.

Be careful with time periods. The renaissance is common, but the Victorian era is proper because it was named after Queen Victoria of England, a real person.

Used in a sentence: John liked his trip to **London, England**. City is a common noun, but we named the city (London, England) so **London, England** is a proper noun and capitalized.

1.3 Concrete Nouns:

Concrete nouns are nouns that can be perceived through the five senses. They are physical, tangible things that can be seen, touched, heard, smelled, or tasted.

Examples include table, guitar, air, and perfume. Some concrete nouns may seem like abstract nouns (clouds, air) but be careful because they are still concrete. You can touch and breathe air and clouds are made of water vapor.

1.4 Abstract Nouns:

Abstract nouns are nouns that cannot be perceived through the five senses. They are ideas, emotions, time periods, or concepts.

Examples include strength, love, happiness, time, consequences, the renaissance, and freedom. Theories such as the theory of relativity, or the big bang theory are counted as abstract nouns.

1.5 Countable (Count) Nouns:

Countable nouns are nouns that can be counted. Simple! They have both singular and plural forms.

Examples include pen (singular) and pens (plural), cow and cows. You can count cars, rabbits, arrows, clouds, and houses.

1.6 Uncountable (Non-Count) Nouns:

Uncountable nouns are nouns that cannot be counted. They do not have a plural form.

Examples include water, rice, butter, and sugar. Although one can say I want three sugars and if they are in packets or in cubes and can get away with it. (Same thing applies with those little individual pats of butter you get in restaurants.) You would probably still say I want two **pats** of butter rather than I want three butters though.

No one orders a rice for example, or says they are going to give the blood. Articles like a, an, and the give the noun away as uncountable if they cannot be used with the noun. You have to be careful and really think about some noncount nouns such as fish. You might say it's a count noun, "I can have a fish for dinner, or I can have two fish for dinner." But think about it. Having a fish for dinner makes it sound like you are planning to dine or eat with a fish as your guest! If you are having fish for dinner, then you are dining (eating) the fish. It's a noncount noun.

1.7 Collective Nouns:

Collective nouns are nouns that are singular but made up of many parts. These nouns have plurals.

Examples include crowd, class, jury, audience, council, group, team, set, kit, flock, herd, and army. (Plurals: groups, flocks, crowds, armies) An army is made up of people, equipment, sometimes animals etc. but we call the whole (collective) thing an army. Think of them as a collection of something. In my opinion we need to use more collective nouns. They're fun. Here are a few examples I like:

A group of owls is called a parliament.

A group of tigers is called an ambush.

A group of cobras is called a quiver.

A group of ravens is called an unkindness.

A group of crows is called a murder.

A group of house cats is called a clowder

A group of Elephants is a memory or a parade.

A group of Rhinos is a crash.

Some collective nouns you know well like:

A pack of dogs, wolves, coyotes, etc.

A pride of lions.

A gaggle of geese.

A school of fish.

You should google collective nouns for animals and look at all the colorful collective examples.

1.8 Compound Nouns:

Compound nouns are when two nouns or a noun and an adjective are put together to make a new noun. Examples include tooth+paste=toothpaste, milk+shake=milkshake, door+bell=doorbell etc. Sometimes the words are not joined together as one word but are still considered one word (or thing) such as in the compound noun water bottle.

Examples include: doorbell, bedroom, living room, light switch, door knob, ice-box, dining room.

1.9 Plurals:

If you have more than one noun and it's a count noun you can usually just add an "S" to it and it's plural (more than one.) If you have a car and you buy another one you simply add an "S" and you have cars. But, like with most English grammar, there are exceptions. If the noun already ends in "S" for example. You cannot add an "S" to bus because it does nothing. Adding an "S" to bus is buss. It's the same word pronunciation and basically does nothing to the word except add an "S" So, if you have a bus and you want to get another bus, you need an "es" (Buses.) Words like glass, bonus, sinus all need an "es."

Words that end in "X" also require "es." box becomes boxes, fox becomes foxes, ax becomes axes, but not ox because ox has an irregular plural; oxen (See next section)

Words that end in "CH" or "SH" also require an "es" church becomes churches, bench becomes benches, dish becomes dishes, wish becomes wishes.

Some nouns that end in "O" also require an "es" such as potato becomes potatoes and tomato becomes tomatoes.

Some plurals do not have or need an "S" or "es." They remain the same whether singular or plural. Many non-count nouns do not change. The plural of the non-count noun butter is not butters but simply just butter. Moose, deer, sheep, and fish are also the same spelling whether singular and plural.

Look at all the deer crossing the road. vs. Look at the deer crossing the road. The word "all" clues the reader in that the word deer in the first sentence is plural. The second sentence is most likely a single deer, but could also be many deer. Reading the second sentence in a paragraph would probably clue the reader in as to how many deer there are crossing the road.

1.10 Irregular plurals:

Words you do not add an "s" or "es" to make them plural. The plural of child is children, octopus is octopi and octopuses (also octopodes because for some reason octopus has three plurals) county becomes counties, cactus becomes cacti. By the way you can find if a word ending in "y" drops the "y" and adds "ies" or keeps the "y" and adds an "s" to make it plural by looking at the letter before the "y." If the letter is a vowel like in toy the plural is toys just add an "s." If the letter is a consonant like army, you drop the "y" and add "ies." Armies. Other irregular plurals include" knife=knives, wife=wives, mouse=mice, and goose=geese.

1.11 Functions of Nouns

Subject:

Nouns can function as the subject of a sentence. They are the main actor in the sentence, and the verb describes their action. For example, "Sarah is singing a song." The sentence is about Sarah

Object:

Nouns can also function as the object of a sentence. They receive the action of the verb. For example, "The dog chased the ball." The ball is receiving the action of being chased.

Possessive:

Nouns can show possession or ownership. For example, "This is Sarah's book." Apostrophe "S" indicates singular possession as in "John's car." "S" apostrophe indicates plural possession as in "the Jones' house." Some nouns already ending in S but are singular nouns get the apostrophe anyway after the S as in "Melias' jacket." It's still singular possessive. It's just weird to write "Melias's Jacket."

People often have trouble with possessive nouns so here are the four rules of possessive nouns. Learn these rules and you should not have any trouble understanding where to put the apostrophe before the "S" or after the "S."

Rule 1: Singular nouns (a person, a place, a thing, or an idea) just add an apostrophe "S" at the end of the noun. (**John's** car is red.)

Rule 2: Singular nouns ending in "S" followed directly by a word beginning with "S" just add an apostrophe after the "S" of the singular noun. **Texas'** students are some of the smartest students in the world. (Yes, I am from Texas!)

Rule 3: Plural nouns ending in "S" just put an apostrophe after the noun. Today we will move all the **students'** desks around the room.

Rule 4: Irregular plural nouns just add an apostrophe "S." It's time to clean the **children's** room. There is a new **men's** clothing store in the strip mall.

Appositive:

Nouns can be used as appositives, which are words that rename or explain another noun in the sentence. For example, "My friend, the doctor, is coming over." "The doctor" is telling or renaming who the friend is. To punctuate appositives the rule is if you need the information in the appositive, you do not need commas and if you don't need the information, you do need commas. Most appositives can be removed, and the sentence still make sense like "My friend is coming over." The sentence still makes sense without the appositive "the doctor" If you need the information, we call this essential or restrictive and if you don't it's called nonessential or nonrestrictive.

Examples:

My wife, Jill, is my best friend. (Jill is nonessential because most people only have one wife or husband so if I say my wife it's going to be Jill. Therefore, I put commas around the appositive Jill)

My sister Connie has five children. (Connie is essential to the meaning of the sentence because I have two sisters. When I write my sister has five children and I have two sisters the reader doesn't know which sister I am referring to, therefore it is essential I name which sister has the five children and since the appositive is essential, I do not need to set it off with commas.)

Okay, there are a lot of things nouns can do. Nouns are an essential part of any language. They are used to name people, places, things, concepts, and ideas. Nouns come in different types, including common, proper, concrete, abstract, countable, uncountable, collective, and compound. Additionally, nouns can function as the subject, object, possessive, or appositive in a sentence. By understanding the different types and functions of nouns, you can enhance your writing and communication skills. Now, on to noun phrases. (after the exercises!)

1.12 Denominal Adjectives

Okay, now that we have looked at nouns and understand them, I need to point out that some adjectives get misclassified as nouns. Look at this sentence:

June had to rush to get onto the city bus before it left without her.

Some might say "city" in this sentence is a noun because the word "city" IS a noun when used by itself. In fact, it's a common noun; however, in this sentence it is describing (modifying) the word bus. Adjectives answer "which one," "what kind", or "how many." If you ask "what kind of bus" the answer is **city** bus. That makes "city" a denominal adjective (an adjective made from a noun.) Other forms of denominal adjectives are proper nouns given a suffix like the word "Dickensian" which is used to indicate nineteenth century London as it is described in the collected works of author Charles Dickens. A Dickensian London is a Victorian London with high poverty rates, workhouses, and debtor's prisons. Do not confuse denominal adjectives as nouns.

Practice Exercises: Write your best answer to the question (write here or on another piece of paper)

    1. What is a common noun?

2. Give an example of a proper noun.

3. What is an abstract noun?

4. What is a concrete noun?

5. What is a collective noun?

6. What is a countable noun?

7. What is a non-countable noun?

8. What is a compound noun?

9. What is a possessive noun?

10. What is a singular noun?

11. What is a plural noun?

12. What is a denominal adjective and why is it not a noun?

Noun Worksheet

Part One | Noun Types

Directions: Read each of the following sentences and determine the noun type of the italicized word.

1. What type of noun is the word *Ford Motor Company* as it is used in the following sentence?

   The Ford Motor Company was started by Henry Ford in the early 1900s.

   a) Proper noun
   b) Plural noun
   c) Common noun
   d) Not a noun

2. What type of noun is the word *car* as it is used in the following sentence?

   The motor car was invented in the late 1800s, but it was not widely manufactured until the turn of the 20ᵗʰ century.

   a) Common noun
   b) Plural noun
   c) Proper noun
   d) Not a noun

3. What type of noun is the word *time* as it is used in the following sentence?

   Time is a relative concept, but had the car been invented in the 1700s, what would cars look like today?

   a) Concrete noun
   b) Proper noun
   c) Abstract noun
   d) Not a noun

4. What type of noun is the word *air* as it is used in the following sentence?

   Because it is believed car exhaust pollutes the air, emissions devices have been invented and installed in all vehicles to reduce the pollution levels.

   a) Concrete noun
   b) Proper noun
   c) Abstract noun
   d) Not a noun

5. Is the word *wheels* a count, possessive, or an uncountable noun as it is used in the following sentence?

   Would you be surprised to learn some early cars had fewer wheels than most cars today?

   a) Uncountable noun
   b) Count noun
   c) Possessive noun
   d) Not a noun

6. Is the word *cars* as it is used in the following sentence a possessive, count, abstract, or noncount noun?

In fact, some of the earlier cars only had three wheels.

a) Noncount noun

b) Abstract noun

c) Possessive noun

d) Count noun

7. Is the word *oil* as it is used in the following sentence a count, noncount, or plural noun?

Because of the invention of the automobile, the need for oil has boomed over the entirety of the 20th century.

a) Count noun

b) Plural noun

c) Noncount noun

d) Not a noun

8. What type of noun is the word *crowds* as it is used in the following sentence?

Crowds of people used to flock to events unveiling new brands and models of cars.

a) Compound noun

b) Abstract noun

c) Possessive noun

d) Collective noun

9. What type of noun is the word *door panels* as it is used in the following sentence?

In the 1970s many car door panels were made to look like real wood.

a) Compound noun

b) Singular noun

c) Possessive noun

d) Collective noun

10. How would you pluralize the noun *shelf*?

a) Add an "S" to the end.

b) Drop the "f" and add "VES."

c) Add "ES" to the end.

d) It's not a noun

11. How would you pluralize the word *country*?

a) Add an "S" to the end.

b) It's not a noun

c) Add "ES" to the end.

d) Drop the "Y" and add "IES."

Part Two | Fill in the Blank

Directions: Choose the answer that best completes the sentences. Circle your response.

12. Many people mistakenly believe Henry Ford invented the _____, which he didn't, but he did improve it.

a) automobiles

b) automobile's

c) automobile

d) automobiles'

13. The automobile, an important invention, has evolved a lot over the past planet 100 _____.

a) year

b) years

c) year's

d) years'

14. The _____ is also an important invention.

a) computers

b) computer's

c) computer

d) computers'

15. Our solar _____ is comprised of 8 planets now that Pluto has been downgraded.

a) System

b) Systems

c) System's

d) Systems'

16. The Lord of the _____ trilogy of books was made into movies by the director Peter Jackson.

a) Rings

b) Ring's

c) Rings'

d) Rings's

17. _____ hat was once shot by a would-be assassin as he was riding through the country side years before John Wilkes Booth did the deed for real in 1865.

a) Abraham Lincoln

b) Abraham Lincoln s

c) Abraham Lincoln's

d) Abraham Lincolns 's

18. The planet Venus was named after the Roman _____ of Love.

a) goddesses

b) goddess's

c) goddess'

d) goddess

19. The planet _____ rotates around the sun so fast the NASA space probe Messenger had to basically catch it before it could take pictures and send them back to Earth.

a) Mercurys'

b) Mercurys

c) Mercury

d) Mercury's

20. Since the beginning of time, _____ quest to explore unknown places has been in full swing.

a) Man

b) Man's

c) Mans's

d) Mans'

Part Three | Functions of Nouns

Directions: Read each of the following sentences and determine the correct function of the *italicized* noun or noun phrase.

21. The automobile, *an important invention,* has evolved a lot over the past 100 years.

a) A participle

b) A possessive noun

c) An appositive

d) A plural noun

22. The sun *drives* our weather here on Earth.

a) Compound noun

b) Possessive noun

c) Not a noun

d) Collective noun

23. A *flock* of birds is flying overhead.

a) Compound Noun
b) Possessive noun
c) Not a noun
d) Collective noun

24. Could you replace the *doorknob* on the front door? The old one has a broken lock.

a) Count noun
b) Compound noun
c) Complex noun
d) Collective noun

25. Jupiter is the largest *planet* in our solar system.

a) Common noun
b) Compound noun
c) Collective noun
d) Proper noun

26. Scientists believe the sun will last for *billions* of years.

a) Not a noun
b) Plural noun
c) Possessive noun
d) Possessive noun

27. Fuel prices have increased over the years due to *inflation* and other factors.

a) plural
b) common
c) singular
d) Both b & c

28. Before the invention of the automobile, the horse and carriage was the *preferred* way to get around.

a) common
b) possessive
c) Not a noun
d) proper

29. The common house cat originated from the *Middle East.*

a) proper
b) concrete
c) abstract
d) Both a & b

30. *Nouns* are one of the most important parts of speech.

a) Noncount noun
b) Not a noun
c) Count noun
d) Possessive noun

Chapter 2

Verbs

Verbs are the action words that give life to a sentence. In this chapter, we'll explore the different types of verbs, their basic tenses, and the rules for using them correctly.

Verbs are the action words of a sentence. They convey an action, occurrence, or state of being. In this chapter, we will explore the definition, types, and functions of verbs.

2.0 Definition of Verbs:

A verb is a word used to express an action, occurrence, or state of being. It is often referred to as the doing word in a sentence. In simpler terms, a verb is a word that describes what is happening in a sentence.

2.1 Types of Verbs:

Action Verbs:

Action verbs are the most common type of verb. They describe a physical or mental action. (Things that can be done) Examples include run, sing, and think.

Action verbs can be transitive or intransitive. Transitive verbs have a direct object receiving their action while intransitive verbs do not.

Auxiliary (helping) Verbs:

Auxiliary verbs, also known as helping verbs, are used to form various verb tenses, questions, and negatives.

There are twenty-three helping verbs. All twenty-three are: am, is, are, was, were, will, be, being, been, has, have, had, do, did, does, may, might, must, shall, should, would, could, and can. Using different helping verbs changes the tense (time something occurs) in a sentence. For Example:

I am leaving today. ("am" indicates present tense.)

I will be leaving today. (Change the helping verbs "am" to "will be" and now it's future tense.)

Irregular Verbs:

Irregular verbs are verbs that do not follow the standard grammar rules for verbs. Normally you can form the past tense of a verb by adding -d, -ed, or -ied, but verbs like "get" for example; you cannot form the simple past tense by adding the standard -d, -ed, or -ied.

You cannot say I geted the lesson the instructor was teaching me. You have to change the verb to got. I got the lesson the instructor was teaching me. It would almost be comical to try to add -d to an irregular verb. "Did you see the comet?" "Yes, I seed it." It should be "Yes, I saw it." An alphabetical list of the most common irregular verbs is included at the end of this chapter.

Linking Verbs:

Linking verbs are used to link the subject of a sentence to a predicate noun or adjective (they tell you something about the subject and are directly related to the subject. John is a fireman. Fireman is telling you what John is. They are linked by the verb "is" John is fireman. They do not show an action but rather a state of being. A state of being means that you and I are "beings" human beings on this planet. I am, you are, refer to you and me as a being. Examples include is, am, and seem.

Linking verbs can look like action verbs sometimes. If you say, "She is looking out the window." "She" is actually doing the "looking" In other words the subject is doing the action of the verb. If you say, "That hamburger looks delicious." Hamburger is the subject but it's not doing the "looking" If your hamburger is looking at you something is very wrong! Since the subject (hamburger) is not doing the verb (looks) you can tell "looks" is a linking verb linking hamburger with delicious.

Here are some verb types/forms to be aware of especially when writing:

Modal Verbs:

Personally, these pop up a lot when I am creative writing. I will have a character say, "We have to do (insert whatever here)" and the word processor wants me to use "must" rather than "have to."

Modal verbs are a kind of helping verb or a helping verb with a preposition (called semi-modals) used to express ability, permission, possibility, or obligation.

Some modal verbs in the English language are:

1. Can/could/be able to

2. May/might

3. Must/have to

4. Shall/should/ought to

5. Will/would

They can be used with different verb tenses (He should find a wife. He will find a wife etc.) They can sometimes sound stiff if you read them out loud, so think about them and use the one that makes the sentence flow.

Stative Verbs:

Stative verbs are verbs that point out a state rather than an action. You can feel with your fingers. Feel is an action . If you are feeling down, you are not physically "feeling" you are instead expressing a state of being.

Another example is if you are seeing someone romantically. Consider:

I am seeing John. He is a great boyfriend. (Seeing as in dating) Seeing is a stative verb here.

Are you seeing John? He is trying to paint that corner and failing! (Seeing with eyes) Seeing is an action verb here.

Phrasal Verbs:

Phrasal verbs are what they sound like, they are verbs with a preposition or a adjective attached. When trying to find the verb in a sentence, students often get confused by these because they want to use the preposition in a phrase that doesn't exist.

Some of these verbs are:

broke down/ broken down

live up to

left out

wake up

deal with

and many more....

The airplane **took off** on time from the airport.

You better hurry; you don't want to be **left out** of the activities.

You need to **wake up** early tomorrow so I can drive you to school.

Notice in the above examples the prepositions are with the verb and do not form or belong to a prepositional phase.

2.2 Functions of Verbs:

Predicate:

Verbs are the main part of the predicate, which is the part of the sentence that describes what the subject is doing or being. For example, "Sarah is singing a song." In fact, you can define the predicate as anything but the subject, or the "verb" part of the sentence. I cried. "I" is the subject and "cried" is the predicate.

Tense:

Verbs can show the tense of a sentence, indicating when an action or state of being occurred. There are actually twelve verb tenses! The common examples of tenses include past, present, and future.

Voice:

Verbs can be either active or passive voice. In active voice, the subject performs the action, while in passive voice, the subject receives the action. For example, "The cat chased the mouse" (active) versus "The mouse was chased by the cat" (passive). We will discuss active and passive voice in more detail in chapter 21.

Mood:

Verbs can also express the mood of a sentence, which indicates the speaker's attitude towards what is being said. Examples of moods include indicative, imperative, and subjunctive. (See chapter 21)

Agreement: (Subject and Verb)

Verbs must agree with their subject in number and person. In other words, a singular subject requires a singular verb, and a plural subject requires a plural verb. For example, "The **cat likes** to meow" (singular) versus "The **cats like** to meow." (plural). Notice the placement of the "S" on the verb in the first sentence, and then on the noun in the second sentence.

Verbs are essential in conveying the action, occurrence, or state of being in a sentence. They come in different types, including action, linking, and auxiliary verbs, and have various functions, such as indicating tense, voice, mood, and agreement. There are a lot more aspects to verbs than I could fit in this one overview chapter, so I gave many of these verb concepts their own chapter in the advanced section beginning with chapter 15.

Practice Exercises: Some questions will require a bit of thought.

1. What is a transitive verb?

a) A verb that does not require an object

b) A verb that requires a direct object

c) A verb that requires an indirect object

2. Which of the following is an example of an intransitive verb? (A verb that cannot have an object receiving its action)

a) to eat

b) to give

c) to think

3. Which of the following is a linking verb?

a) to run

b) to jump

c) to be

4. Which of the following is an example of a helping verb?

a) is

b) eat

c) run

5. Which of the following is an example of an action verb?

a) to walk

b) to love

c) to hope

The following pages include the complete list of irregular verbs with their plural and past participle forms.

Irregular Verbs – Complete List

Base Form	Past Simple	Past Participle
arise	arose	arisen
awake	awoke	awoken
be	was/were	been
bear	bore	born(e)
beat	beat	beaten
become	became	become
begin	began	begun
bend	bent	bent
bet	bet	bet
bind	bound	bound
bite	bit	bitten

Base Form	Past Simple	Past Participle
bleed	bled	bled
blow	blew	blown
break	broke	broken
breed	bred	bred
bring	brought	brought
broadcast	broadcast	broadcast
build	built	built
burn	burnt/burned	burnt/burned
burst	burst	burst
buy	bought	bought
can	could	... (been able)
catch	caught	caught

Base Form	Past Simple	Past Participle
choose	chose	chosen
cling	clung	clung
come	came	come
cost	cost	cost
creep	crept	crept
cut	cut	cut
deal	dealt	dealt
dig	dug	dug
do	did	done
draw	drew	drawn
dream	dreamt/dreamed	dreamt/dreamed
drink	drank	drunk

Base Form	Past Simple	Past Participle
drive	drove	driven
eat	ate	eaten
fall	fell	fallen
feed	fed	fed
feel	felt	felt
fight	fought	fought
find	found	found
fly	flew	flown
forbid	forbade	forbidden
forget	forgot	forgotten
forgive	forgave	forgiven
freeze	froze	frozen

Base Form	Past Simple	Past Participle
get	got	got
give	gave	given
go	went	gone
grind	ground	ground
grow	grew	grown
hang	hung	hung
have	had	had
hear	heard	heard
hide	hid	hidden
hit	hit	hit
hold	held	held
hurt	hurt	hurt

Base Form	Past Simple	Past Participle
keep	kept	kept
kneel	knelt	knelt
know	knew	known
lay	laid	laid
lead	led	led
lean	leant/leaned	leant/leaned
learn	learnt/learned	learnt/learned
leave	left	left
lend	lent	lent
lie (in bed)	lay	lain
lie (to not tell the truth)	lied	lied
light	lit/lighted	lit/lighted

Base Form	Past Simple	Past Participle
lose	lost	lost
make	made	made
may	might	...
mean	meant	meant
meet	met	met
mow	mowed	mown/mowed
must	had to	...
overtake	overtook	overtaken
pay	paid	paid
put	put	put
read	read	read
ride	rode	ridden

Base Form	Past Simple	Past Participle
ring	rang	rung
rise	rose	risen
run	ran	run
saw	sawed	sawn/sawed
say	said	said
see	saw	seen
sell	sold	sold
send	sent	sent
set	set	set
sew	sewed	sewn/sewed
shake	shook	shaken
shall	should	...

Base Form	Past Simple	Past Participle
shed	shed	shed
shine	shone	shone
shoot	shot	shot
show	showed	shown
shrink	shrank	shrunk
shut	shut	shut
sing	sang	sung
sink	sank	sunk
sit	sat	sat
sleep	slept	slept
slide	slid	slid
smell	smelt	smelt

Base Form	Past Simple	Past Participle
sow	sowed	sown/sowed
speak	spoke	spoken
spell	spelt/spelled	spelt/spelled
spend	spent	spent
spill	spilt/spilled	spilt/spilled
spin	spun	spun
spit	spat	spat
spread	spread	spread
stand	stood	stood
steal	stole	stolen
stick	stuck	stuck
sting	stung	stung

Base Form	Past Simple	Past Participle
stink	stank	stunk
strike	struck	struck
swear	swore	sworn
sweep	swept	swept
swell	swelled	swollen/swelled
swim	swam	swum
swing	swung	swung
take	took	taken
teach	taught	taught
tear	tore	torn
tell	told	told
think	thought	thought

Base Form	Past Simple	Past Participle
throw	threw	thrown
understand	understood	understood
wake	woke	woken
wear	wore	worn
weep	wept	wept
will	would	...
win	won	won
wind	wound	wound
write	wrote	written

Verbs, Infinitives, Gerunds

Directions: Read each of the following sentences. **Determine which word is functioning as an action verb.** Circle your answer.

1. The boy adjusted the bill of his shredded baseball cap.

a) shredded

b) bill

c) adjusted

d) baseball

2. The red dog tired himself out.

a) tired

b) out

c) dog

d) himself

3. The orange cat tired herself out by playing with the bouncing ball.

a) tired

b) playing

c) bouncing

d) Both a & b

4. The nimble cat chased the mouse into the burning house.

a) burning

b) nimble

c) chased

d) house

5. The pirate ship plowed through the turbulent waters.

a) turbulent

b) plowed

c) through

d) waters

6. The chicken noodle soup tasted delicious against the cold of the day.

a) tasted

b) against

c) delicious

d) soup

7. Winning the marathon, Fred danced with joy at the finish line.

a) winning

b) danced

c) marathon

d) joy

8. After the storm subsided, John shoveled the snow from his driveway.

a) subsided

b) driveway

c) shoveled

d) Both a & c

9. John plans on driving his truck in the town parade.

a) parade   b) driving

c) plans   d) John

Part 2 Verbs of Being (be verbs)

Directions: Read each of the following sentences. **Determine which word is functioning as a verb of being.** Circle your answer.

10.   Stealing and lying are wrong.

a) stealing   b) are

c) lying   d) All of the above

11.   Jill was the first one to run back into the burning building.

a) was   b) run

c) burning   d) building

12.   Is that the soda Helen was drinking?

a) drinking   b) was

c) is   d) was drinking

13.   He is my friend no matter what.

a) is   b) what

c) matter   d) my

14.   Jill is my friend and Jack is yours.

a) yours   b) and

c) friend   d) Is x 2

15.   The guy wearing the purple shirt was my friend for the longest time.

a) wearing   b) was

c) purple   d) for

16.   That man has been a good person all his life.

a) has   b) all

c) has been   d) been

17.   You are impossible to talk to today.

a) talk

b) are

c) today

d) impossible

18. The man with the wagon is the father of the child with the speech impediment.

a) with

b) impediment

c) of

d) is

19. You are my best friend because you have always supported me.

a) supported

b) are

c) have

d) always

20. The car with the rotting tire is my dream car.

a) dream

b) with

c) is

d) rotting

Part 3 Gerunds

Directions: Read each of the following sentences. **Determine which word is functioning as a Gerund.** Circle your answer.

21. John plans on driving his truck in the town parade.

a) plans

b) parade

c) truck

d) driving

22. Eating pizza after sports is fun.

a) is

b) eating

c) sports

d) after

23. Driving racecars must be a lot of fun!

a) driving

b) fun

c) must be

d) a lot

24. I am really not good at running.

a) am

b) really

c) running

d) at

25. Jumping off the cliff and diving into the ocean is awesome!

a) diving

b) Jumping

c) is

d) Both a & c

Part 3 Infinitives

Directions: Read each of the following sentences. **Determine which word is functioning as an Infinitive.** Circle your answer.

26. It's time to water the plants.

a) plants

b) time

c) to water

d) no infinitive

27. The crew of the ship couldn't wait to jump from the ship into the water.

a) couldn't wait

b) into the water

c) of

d) to jump

28. I don't like to run in marathons.

a) run

b) in

c) do not

d) to run

29. It's best to let the subject die.

a) is best

b) to let

c) die

d) it is

30. John likes to fish directly off the dock.

a) to fish

b) off

c) directly

d) likes

Chapter 3

Pronouns

No, a pronoun is not a noun that has gone pro! (sorry, dad joke) We use pronouns to take the place of nouns, so we don't have to repeat those nouns over and over and over again in the sentence. When I was teaching grammar in public school, pronouns were the toughest part of speech for students to get right for some reason. (Advanced grammar is a different story)

Pronouns are an essential part of language that replaces a noun or noun phrase in a sentence. In this chapter, we will explore the definition, types, and functions of pronouns.

3.0 Definition of Pronouns:

A pronoun is a word that replaces a noun or noun phrase in a sentence. It is often referred to as a substitute word. In simpler terms, a pronoun is a word used to avoid repeating a noun or noun phrase. (I've said that three times now. Research shows it takes three times to sink in, so you should know a pronoun takes the place of a noun by now, right?)

3.1 Types of Pronouns:

Personal Pronouns:

Personal pronouns refer to people, places, or things. They come in three forms: first-person (I, we), second-person (you), and third-person (he, she, it, they). When we look at pronouns in the first, second, and third person we call that the

perspective of the pronoun. If the pronoun is a subject of a sentence we call it the **subjective case pronoun,** and if a pronoun is the object of a sentence we call that the **objective case pronoun.**

Example: "She kissed him on the lips." "She" is the subjective case pronoun and "him" is the objective case pronoun. They are not interchangeable. She is always subjective case and him is always objective case. In other words you cannot say: "Him kissed she on the lips," because the pronoun cases are not correct. (See section 3.2 Pronoun Cases for more.)

Demonstrative Pronouns:

Demonstrative pronouns are used to point to or identify a specific person, place, or thing. Examples include this, that, these, and those.

Oh, I like **this**.

I have a bad feeling about **this**.

These are really cool, but **those** are weird.

I have seen people call demonstrative pronouns other parts of speech, and even say they are not pronouns at all. Remember, pronouns take the place of nouns. Demonstrative pronouns **ARE** taking the place of nouns. The noun is simply not present in the sentence. If you say I like ice cream, ice cream is a noun. If you take a bite of the ice cream and say "Oh, I like this a lot." You are replacing the noun ice cream with "this", a demonstrative pronoun.

Indefinite Pronouns:

Indefinite pronouns are used to refer to people or things that are not specific. Examples include anyone, someone, and everything.

Would **anyone** like a soda? The question is being asked to every person present and not to one in specific person making it in definite. The noun anyone is replacing is the person or persons who take the speaker up on getting a soda. Anyone could be any person present.

Surely **someone** knows who the killer is.

Relative Pronouns:

Relative pronouns are used to link a clause to a noun or pronoun. They include who, whom, whose, which, and that. Words like "that" should be read to see if they belong in the sentence. Many times, you can just delete the word "that." This is the coffee that I like to buy. Instead, the sentence flows better like this: This is the coffee I like to buy. I call people who overuse "that" as having "that" disease.

The chair, **which** sits in the hallway, belongs to an old set. Which is relatively replacing chair.

The person **who** called me an idiot is an idiot. Who is relatively replacing person.

Interrogative Pronouns:

Interrogative pronouns are used to ask questions. Examples include who, whom, whose, which, and what. The word "Interrogative" shares the same root word with the word "interrogate." (questioning someone)

Who will RSVP for the party do you think?

Whose car is that parked by mine? (There is no such possessive word as who's. If you see the word who's, it is a contraction of who is and does not show any kind of ownership.)

What did you find in there?

If you have trouble with sentences like "Who is your friend." or "You are friends with whom?" on whether to use who or whom, look at section 3.2 about pronoun cases. "Who" is subjective case. "Whom" is objective case. People get confused with interrogative sentences using whom like "To whom are you referring?" Because it looks like whom is in the subjective case but it's still objective. To see it more clearly, change the interrogative into a declarative sentence "You are referring to whom." Now you can see the word "whom" is still objective even when the sentence is arranged in interrogative form.

3.2 Pronoun Cases:

Perspective	Subjective	Objective	Possessive
1st-Person Plural	I We	Me Us	My, Mine Our, Ours
2nd-Person	You	You	Your
3rd-Person Plural	He, She, It They	Him, Her, It Them	His, Hers Their

All right, here are the keys to the kingdom. (My way of saying here is the information that will help you forever with pronouns)

I have already taught you a little about subjects and objects when we did nouns but here is a refresher:

Subjects interact with verbs and do the action.

Objects do no action and often receive the action of the verb.

He yelled at her. (He is the subject doing the yelling. She is the object receiving the action of being yelled at.)

She told on him. (She is the subject doing the action. He is the object receiving the action.)

We call the pronoun doing the action (the subject) subjective case (sometimes called the nominative case.) And the object we call the objective case pronoun. They are not interchangeable. You will never say Him told on she. Because she is subjective case and can only be used as a subject. Him is objective case and can only be used as an object.

Knowing the cases I is subjective and me is objective. So, this is how they work:

He and she are my friends. Or They are my friends using the plural subjective pronoun.

I am friends with him and her. Or I am friends with them.

Since I is subjective and me is objective, I interacts with the verb where me does not. Dad and **I** went fishing. Would you like to go fishing with dad and **me**?

If you get confused do this:

Is it She wants to talk to John and I or She wants to talk to John and me? It's me because it is objective case. It's never She wants to talk to John and I. because I is subjective and cannot be in the objective case. That would be like saying "She wants to talk to I." If you are ever confused on which pronoun to use in which case just substitute the pronoun by itself and use it with the sentence's verb. (I want, me want, talk to I, talk to me) Same goes with My brother and me like to hang out on Saturday nights. Since me is objective and not subjective, using it this way is the same as saying "Me like to hang out on Saturday nights. Me doesn't work in the subjective case so even if you put my "brother and" in front of "me" it still doesn't work.

Let's do the plural.

Is it The principal scolded us teachers or the principal scolded we teachers?

End with the pronoun and it will become clear: The principal scolded us. (yes) The principal scolded we. (no)

Dad and I went fishing. Or Dad and me went fishing. Remove the noun "Dad" and the word "and" and just use the pronoun with the verb to reveal the correct pronoun.

I went fishing. (yes) Me went fishing. (no)

As I stated previously, this will also clear up who and whom for you. Remember: who is subjective and whom is objective.

Who is your friend?

"You are friends with whom?"

Possessive nouns have 's or s' while possessive case pronouns do not have apostrophes at all. Again, there are no apostrophes with pronouns. "It's" is a contraction of it is and not a pronoun. Possessive case pronouns show owner-ship just like possessive nouns. Some of the possessive pronouns include my, mine, ours, their, theirs, hers, his, and its.

Consider this sentence: Samantha and Frederick didn't finish their dinner.

I have seen supposed grammar experts say this sentence is wrong, but it's one hundred percent correct. "Their" is a plural possessive pronoun taking the place of the compound subject "Samantha and Frederick." They together are the "their." In other words, "their" is the pronoun and "Samantha and Frederick" are the antecedent of their. Since there are two subjects, the pronoun and antecedent must agree, so their is in agreement as a plural pronoun. This written entry I saw also said "dinner" should be "dinners" unless the two are eating off the same plate. The author of the piece was wrong again. Dinner is a **collective** noun. It is one thing made up of several foods, utensils, glasses etc. It is singular in this case. To put dinners would mean the two went to more than one separate dinner together and didn't finish either of them.

3.3 Review of the Functions of Pronouns:

Substitution:

Pronouns are used to replace nouns or noun phrases in a sentence. We substitute them for nouns, so we do not have to repeat the noun over and over.

For example, "Sarah loves her cat" (the pronoun her replaces the noun Sarah).

Agreement:

Pronouns must agree in number and gender with the noun they are replacing. For example, "The cat ate its food." (the pronoun its agrees with the singular noun cat. If you know the gender of the animal, you could also say The cat ate her/his food.) You cannot say or write "The cat ate their food." Because cat is singular and their is plural. The pronoun "its" **never** has an apostrophe (It's is a contraction of it is) It usually refers to animals you do not know the gender of like a badger. I am not about to pick up a badger to see if it's a boy or a girl. I am just going to call it an it!

Clarity:

Pronouns are used to avoid repetitive language and to make sentences more clear and concise. For example, "Sarah went to the store, and she bought some bread" (the pronoun she avoids repeating Sarah's name.) Can you imagine repeating proper nouns like names? Sarah went to the store, and Sarah bought some bread. Sarah wanted to make Sarah a sandwich when Sarah got home to Sarah's house. Yikes! Pronouns are a good thing!

Antecedent:

The noun a pronoun refers to (takes the place of) is called its antecedent. (ante means before) For example, "Sarah loves her cat. It is very cute" (the antecedent for the pronoun "her" is Sarah and for the pronoun "it" the antecedent is cat).

Pronouns are essential. Without them just talking would be a laborious task. They come in different types, including personal, demonstrative, indefinite, relative, and interrogative. Pronouns have various functions, such as substitution, agreement, clarity, and antecedent.

If the word doesn't replace a noun in some way, it is not a pronoun. Some words identified here as a pronoun can be other parts of speech as well. The word "that" for example can also be a subordinating conjunction. (see section 10.2)

Practice Exercises:

Multiple Choice Questions:

1. What is a pronoun?

a) A word that describes an action.

b) A word that describes a noun.

c) A word that takes the place of a noun.

2. Which of the following is NOT a type of pronoun?

a) Reflexive

b) Demonstrative

c) Abstract

3. Which pronoun is used to refer to the speaker or writer?

a) You

b) He

c) They

d) We

4. Which pronoun is used to refer to a person or thing that is not specifically named?

a) It

b) They

c) You

d) He

5. Which pronoun is used to show possession?

a) Me

b) Myself

c) Their

d) Its

6. Which pronoun is used to refer to a non-specific person or thing?

a) She

b) They

c) He

d) It

7. Which pronoun is used to refer to a group of people or things?

a) You

b) We

c) It

d) They

8. Which pronoun is used to refer to a person or thing previously mentioned or easily identified?

a) It

b) He

c) She

d) They

9. Which pronoun is used to refer to a female person or animal?

a) He

b) She

c) They

d) It

10. Which pronoun is used to refer to a male person or animal?

a) She

b) It

c) He

d) They

11. Which pronoun is used to refer to a person or thing in a place or position previously mentioned or understood?

a) It

b) They

c) He

d) She

12. Which pronoun is used to refer to the person or thing being addressed?

a) You

b) It

c) He

d) They

13. Which pronoun is used to refer to two people or things?

a) He

b) She

c) They

d) It

14. Which pronoun is used to refer to three or more people or things?

a) He

b) She

c) They

d) It

15. Which pronoun is used to emphasize a noun or pronoun previously mentioned?

a) It

b) He

c) She

d) They

Pronouns case and Perspective questions:

1. What is the subjective (nominative) case of pronouns?

2. When do you use the objective case of pronouns?

3. What is the possessive case of pronouns?

4. What is the difference between first-person, second-person, and third-person perspective?

5. How do you determine the appropriate pronoun case and perspective to use in a sentence?

Pronouns and Antecedents

Part One | Pronouns

Directions: Read each of the following sentences and determine which word is a pronoun based on your options. Circle your answer.

1. Jimmy lost his iPod while hiking in Death Valley.

a) Jimmy
b) in
c) his
d) iPod

2. Fred and Jill met after their first semester in college.

a) their
b) Fred and Jill
c) after
d) college

3. Jane was the one who accused Johnathan of taking the mixed nuts from the table.

a) was
b) who
c) accused
d) one

4. Samantha tried to throw the ball through the hoop, but it hit the side and bounced off the rim.

a) Samantha
b) throw
c) side
d) it

5. John watched as the rattlesnake slithered along the ground, "You don't want to mess with that thing!"

a) John
b) You
c) slithered
d) don't

6. Mark pointed the wrench on the hood of the car, "Could you hand me that?"

a) Mark
b) that
c) you
d) Both b & c

7. Bill used to live in the house alone until he invited his girlfriend to move in last week.

a) Bill
b) girlfriend
c) he
d) until

8. Granny cooks the best food I have ever eaten!

a) I   b) food

c) cooks   d) Granny

9. Helen admired the wild geese as they flew overhead.

a) Helen   b) they

c) flew   d) geese

10.   Fill the gas can until it is three quarters full.

a) it   b) Gas can

c) fill   d) full

11.   Uncle Gerald loved the 1965 Ford Thunderbird and always wanted to own one.

a) loved   b) own

c) Uncle Gerald   d) one

12.   Uncle Gerald finally bought a 1965 Ford Thunderbird when he saved enough money.

a) enough   b) when

c) he   d) money

13.   Get rid of all your troubles while soaking in a relaxing hot tub!

a) rid   b) your

c) all   d) relaxing

Part Two | Antecedents

Directions: Read each of the following sentences and determine which word is an antecedent. Circle your answer.

14.   Jason played in the arcade by himself and racked up a high score at pinball.

a) Jason   b) pinball

c) played   d) Arcade

15.   Sarah chipped a nail while trying to change the oil in her car.

a) her   b) Sarah

c) chipped   d) car

16.   Rob forgot the keys to the shed at home but retrieved them just in time before reporting for
      work.

a) time   b) forgot

c) work   d) keys

17. Drew arrived at the grocery store but was disappointed to find it closed for the day.

a) Drew

b) arrived

c) grocery store

d) to

18. Shawn and Michelle were worried they would be late to the dance, but they actually arrived before the others.

a) were worried

b) late

c) others

d) Shawn and Michelle

19. Dalton caught a man trying to steal a car from off the street, so he called the police to come investigate.

a) Dalton

b) street

c) steal

d) police

20. Debbie and Jack drove to the donut shop early and arrived just before it opened for the day.

a) Debbie and Jack

b) donut shop

c) opened

d) early

Chapter 4
Adjectives

Adjectives and adverbs are the descriptive words that add color and nuance to a sentence. In this chapter, we'll discuss the different types of adjectives and adverbs, their functions, and the rules for using them correctly. We'll also provide examples and exercises to help you practice using them effectively.

4.0 Adjectives

Adjectives are words that modify or describe nouns or pronouns by providing more information about their size, shape, color, age, origin, material, or any other quality that can be attributed to them. (In English grammar we use describe and modify synonymously. They mean the same thing. The red ball bounced high in the air. Red is describing or modifying ball and high is describing or modifying bounced. Adjectives answer which one, what kind, and how many.

There are ten apples in the bag. (How many apples? ten is the adjective)

Look at all the blue marbles. (Which marbles? The blue ones. Blue is the adjective)

I have many red shirts. (what kind of shirt? red is the adjective)

Another example: "The red car is parked outside," the adjective "red" modifies/describes the noun "car" by specifying its color.

Adjectives can be placed either before or after the noun they modify. When they come before the noun, they are called attributive adjectives, and when they come after the noun, they are called predicative adjectives. For example, "a blue sky" is an example of an attributive adjective, while "The sky is blue" is an example of a predicative adjective. Yep, over-complicate it! But at least now you know.

Adjectives can also be compared using three degrees of comparison: positive, comparative, and superlative. The positive degree is used to describe one thing without comparison, such as "big," "small," "happy," or "sad." The comparative degree is used to compare two things and indicate which is superior, using "-er" or "more," such as "bigger," "smaller," "happier," or "sadder." The superlative degree is used to compare more than two things and indicate which is the highest or the most, using "-est" or "most," such as "biggest," "smallest," "happiest," or "saddest."

4.1 Denominal Adjectives

By now you should recognize the root word "nom" it mean name. It's the same as nominate, nomenclature, and nominal. Denominal Adjectives are adjective derived from nouns. Remember, adjectives describe nouns and pronouns, so a denominal adjective would be like The **American** president visited the country. American is a noun but in this case it's modifying (describing) president. It is a denominal adjective.

I have a **Russian** wife.

The **French** people love their cafes.

I just exited the **school** bus.

You are a **loyal** friend. (loyal used here is an abstract noun)

I have seen grammar books confuse these adjectives for nouns, so if you are unsure ask yourself what kind, which one, or how many of the noun in question and the answer will point to the adjective. Which friend? The loyal one. Loyal is the adjective. What kind of wife? A Russian one. Russian is the adjective. But if you say My wife is Russian then Russian would not be an adjective because it isn't describing the wife, it's telling you who she is and is therefore a noun.

4.2 Adjectives of Comparison

In addition to describing nouns, some adjectives show the position of comparison on a scale of positive, comparative, and superlative.

For example: Positive   Comparative   Superlative

   The mountains are **far** away.   The mountains are **farther** than the beach.   These are the **farthest** mountains.

   My sister is a **good** typist.   My sister is a **better** typist than my brother.   My sister is the **best** typist.

   This is a **long** movie.   This movie is **longer** than the last one.   This is the **longest** movie.

 The knight is a **worthy** opponent.   The knight is a **more worthy** opponent than his friend.   The knight is the **most worthy**.

Comparative

The comparative form can be formed by either adding the suffix **-er** or by adding the word **more** before the adjective as illustrated in the 4th example above.

Superlative

The superlative form can be formed by either adding the suffix **-est** or by adding the word **most** before the adjective as illustrated in the 4th example above.

This is why in many yearbooks the catagories such as "The most likely to succeed, the most handsome, and the prettiest" are known as superlatives.

Exceptions

Some adjectives have irregular forms similiar to irregular verb forms.

For example:	Positive	Comparative	Superlative
	good	better	best
	little	less	least
	bad	worse	worst
	much-many-some	more	most T

4.3 Compound Adjectives

When two or more adjectives are joined together to modify the same noun, we call it a compound adjective.

Examples: The can of soda was **freezing cold**. That was a **surprisingly good** lobster dinner. This is a **brightly-lit** hallway. We should all strive to be **open-minded** people.

4.4 Common Mistakes with Adjectives

Fewer vs. Less

Less is the comparative form of little. It should be used with noncount nouns. Fewer is the comparative of few and should be used before plural nouns.

Examples: I can leave work in **less** than an hour.

I have **fewer** candy bars today than I did yesterday.

Farther vs. Further

Farther is used to indicate actual, physical distance. Further is used to indicate figurative or metaphorical distance.

Examples: How much farther do we have to drive?

You went much further with that joke than I think you intended.

Much vs. Many

Use **much** with noncount nouns and **many** with countable nouns. Examples: I don't have **much** butter left.

How **many** children do you have?

Exercises:

Part I: Underline the correct word(s) in the parentheses.

1. In ancient Roman times, salt was once (more valued, most valued) than silver.

2. It is (good, better) to ask a person for help than to receive it.

3. Our new boss is (more kind, kinder) than the last.

4. The (little, less) time I spend playing my guitar, the more guilty I feel.

Part II: Underline the adjective that modifies the bolded noun in each sentence.

1. The kind **grandma** made cookies.

2. The quick **rabbit** hopped across the road.

3. The little **boy** sang the song beautifully.

4. Those red flashing **sirens** are annoying.

5. An old **dog** barked at the moon.

Part III: Underline the group of words in the parentheses that show the adjective(s) in

their correct order.

1. The (very quick bunny, quick very bunny) hopped across the road.

2. At the bar, Jodi sang a/an (American classic, classic American) song for Karaoke Night.

3. The incessant noise of the police siren is very (annoying, annoyed).

4. The long day of teaching left Jill feeling (exhausting, exhausted).

5. Crazy Feather wore a (leather black jacket, black leather jacket) to the ceremonial dance.

Chapter 5
Adverbs

5.0 Adverbs

Adverbs are words that modify or describe verbs, adjectives, and other adverbs. They answer when, how, where, in what way, and to what extent.

The horror film audience often screams at the scary parts. (when do they scream? often is the adverb)

The boy ran quickly. (how did he run? quickly is the adverb)

Adverbs can be formed by adding the suffix "-ly" to an adjective.

Adverbs can also be compared using the same three degrees of comparison as adjectives. The positive degree is used to describe the manner or degree of the action or quality without comparison.

Some adverbs are called intensifiers because they kick it up a notch. Really and very are intensifiers and should be used sparingly. He ran fast. He ran very fast is kicking it up a notch, but he ran very, very, very fast is abusing it a bit!

Just like most of the parts of speech, you can over complicate adverbs. Just keep in mind they usually describe verbs, adjectives and other adverbs and you will be fine.

5.1 Adverbs of Manner

The adverb of manner explains how an action is carried out. These are the adverbs that usually end in -ly. (but not always. Yes, there are exceptions) About 80% of adverbs you find in sentences end in -ly.

Examples include badly, slowly, sweetly, warmly, sadly, etc.

The boat ride in the park went badly.

The old lady sadly passed away.

The girl clumsily stumbled into the room.

5.2 Adverbs of Purpose (or Reason)

These adverbs help tell "why" something is occurring.

I bought insurance **so that** my family is protected if I die.

I brought you a present **since** it's your birthday.

5.3 Adverbs of Place

Adverbs of place tell where an action happens, or they at least help explain where an action happens. These adverbs rarely end in -ly as you might expect of most adverbs.

Common adverbs of place include: around, by, back, close by, left, up, down, everywhere, and the directions such as north, west, east, and south and their other forms like northeast etc. The can be of direction, distance, or position.

Direction

South Carolina is located **south** of New York.

The skier tumbled **down** the slope.

I looked for my keys **everywhere**.

Distance

His girlfriend broke up with him and moved **far away.**

Don't stand so **close** to me.

I saw a bigfoot walking **over there**!

Position

The cat hid **underneath** the bed.

Move **forward** to the front of the line, please.

5.4 Adverbs of Frequency

Adverbs that express time or intervals of time. They can tell us how often something happens.

Adverbs **usually** end with the suffix -ly but not always.

Teachers **normally** have good judgement and morals.

The old professor **always** loves teaching new students.

5.5 Adverbs of Time

You might think these fall under adverbs of Frequency and they are similar but adverbs of time tell us "when" something happens.

I just saw you **yesterday** and now I'm seeing you **today** as well.

You said you were leaving **last minute**.

You need to leave **now.**

Exercises:

In the following sentences underline the adverbs and state their kind.

    1. The bird sang cheerfully. Adverb Kind _____

    2. What is your father doing outside? Adverb Kind _____

3. John practices guitar four times every day. Adverb Kind _____

4. We will let you know about the job soon. Adverb Kind _____

5. The turtle crawled slowly. Adverb Kind _____

6. The ghosts are haunting there. Adverb Kind _____

7. The machine usually comes on automatically. Adverb Kind _____

8. The woman took her bow gracefully. Adverb Kind _____

9. he bugs were flying everywhere. Adverb Kind_____

Adjective or Adverb?

Directions: Choose the pair of words that BEST completes each sentence.
Remember, **adjectives** modify **nouns** and **pronouns** and **adverbs** modify
verbs, adjectives, and other **adverbs.**

1. Paul responded _____ to the _____ data collected by his staff.

a) negatively, negatively   b) negative, negatively

c) negatively, negative   d) negative, negative

2. The professor delivered the lecture in a _____ yet confident manner while also being
    _____ passionate about his subject matter.

a) calm, fierce   b) calm, fiercely

c) calmly, fierce   d) calmly, fiercely

3. The baseball spun _____ as it sailed through the air cutting through the _____ breeze.

a) wild, gentle   b) wild, gently

c) wildly, gently   d) wildly, gentle

4. Ryan, the racecar driver, drove _____ yet _____ as he rounded the final curve to the
    finish line.

a) bold, reckless   b) bold, recklessly

c) boldly, reckless   d) boldly, recklessly

5. Jill was impressed by the _____ light show but was less than enthused by the _____ noise
    off the surrounding buildings.

a) echo, dazzling   b) echoing, determined

c) dazzling, echoing   d) dazzlingly, exacting

6. A _____ wind blew through the trees then whistled along the _____ street.

a) haunting, lonely   b) hauntingly, deservedly

c) haunted, lone   d) elegantly, lonely

7. The _____ water flowed through the hollow log from the _____ snows in the mountains.

a) heavy, purely   b) purely, heavily

c) pure, heavy   d) heavily, purely

8. Jed was a _____ man, so he _____ spoke until he listened to all sides first.

a) rare, patiently   b) patient, rarely

c) large, rapidly   d) stoic, patiently

9. The car spun _____ out of control until the driver _____ corrected it.

a) quickly, rapid   b) rapidly, quickly

c) rapid, quick   d) quick, rapidly

10. The captain _____ navigated the cargo ship through the _____ waters.

a) safely, treacherous   b) safe, treacherously

c) treacherous, safe   d) treacherously, safe

11. John was not feeling _____, so he was not having a very _____ day.

a) well, goodly   b) good, well

c) stiff, well   d) well, good

12. Ricky was _____ for the _____ gift his wife had sent to him.

a) thankful, unique   b) thank, uniquely

c) uniquely, thank   d) unique, thankful

13. The rock face was formed in a _____ pattern onto the _____ cliffside.

a) uniformly, dusty   b) uniform, dustily

c) uniform, dusty   d) uniformly, dustily

14. The _____ suit in Ryan's closet _____ got worn.

a) blue, barely   b) tailored, hardly

c) tailored, rarely   d) all options would work as Adjectives and Adverbs

15. The _____ bridge was always _____ in the winter.

a) icy, late   b) huge, icy

c) long, lately   d) hugely, broken

Chapter 6

Interjections

Interjections are short exclamations or expressions of emotion that are often used to convey a speaker's feelings or attitudes towards a particular situation or event. They are not grammatically connected to the rest of the sentence, but rather stand alone as independent words or phrases before the beginning of the sentence. They should not be used with academic writing, but they are nearly essential to creative writing and dialogue. If the emotion is strong, they are punctuated with a exclamation point, a comma if the feeling is not as strong.

6.0 Interjections

6.1 Types of Interjections

Interjections come in a variety of forms and can be classified into several different categories based on their meaning or usage. Some common types of interjections include:

Expressions of surprise or shock:

Oh! Wow! Yikes! Ouch! Holy cow!

Expressions of joy or happiness:

Yay! Hooray! Bravo! Woohoo! Awesome!

Expressions of disgust or disapproval:

Ugh! Gross! Blech! Yuck! Ew!

Expressions of agreement or acknowledgement:

Yes! Okay! Alright! Indeed! Absolutely!

Usage of Interjections

Interjections can be used in a variety of ways, depending on the speaker's intention or purpose. Some common uses of interjections include:

Expressing emotions or reactions: Interjections are often used to express a speaker's emotions or reactions to a particular situation or event. For example, "Oh no! I forgot my keys!" conveys the speaker's sense of disappointment or frustration at having forgotten their keys.

Adding emphasis: Interjections can also be used to add emphasis or emphasis to a statement or sentence. For example, "Wow, that was an incredible performance!" conveys the speaker's sense of amazement or admiration.

Introducing a statement or idea: Interjections can also be used to introduce a statement or idea, particularly in informal or conversational contexts. For example, "Hey, did you hear about the new restaurant that just opened?" serves as an introduction to the speaker's statement about the new restaurant. Be sure not to overuse when writing creatively.

It is important to note that while interjections can add color and emotion to language, they should be used sparingly and appropriately. There really isn't much to remember rule-wise about this part of speech. It's easy to punctuate (Exclamation if the emotion is strong, a comma if the emotion is weaker) and it's easy to spot when editing. However, the overuse of interjections can make writing or speech seem unprofessional or juvenile. If you noticed in the examples above interjections tend to be used almost exclusively in dialogue good for you!

Practice Exercises:

1. What is an interjection?

a) A type of sentence

b) A part of speech

c) A form of punctuation

2. Which of the following is an example of an interjection?

a) The cat jumped over the fence

b) Wow!

c) I am going to the store

3. Which of the following interjections expresses surprise?

a) Hurray!

b) Oops!

c) Wow!

4. Which of the following interjections expresses agreement?

a) Ugh!

b) Yeah!

c) Oops!

5. Which of the following interjections expresses disapproval?

a) Yay!

b) Oh no!

c) Ahem!

6. Which of the following interjections is used to get someone's attention?

a) Oh no!

b) Ahem!

c) Hurray!

7. Which of the following interjections is used to express relief?

a) Hurray!

b) Phew!

c) Oops!

8. Which of the following interjections is used to express happiness?

a) Ugh!

b) Yay!

c) Oops!

9. Which of the following interjections is used to express sympathy?

a) Oops!

b) Aww!

c) Yay!

10. Which of the following interjections is used to express anger?

a) Oh no!

b) Ugh!

c) Yay!

11. Which of the following interjections is used to express excitement?

a) Oops!

b) Yay!

c) Ahem!

12. Which of the following interjections is used to express doubt?

a) Hmm...

b) Yay!

c) Oops!

13. Which of the following interjections is used to express frustration?

a) Oops!

b) Ugh!

c) Yay!

14. Which of the following interjections is used to express admiration?

a) Wow!

b) Ugh!

c) Phew!

15. Which of the following interjections is used to express gratitude?

a) Oops!

b) Thank you!

c) Ahem!

Interjections Worksheet

Directions: Choose the interjection that best completes the sentence. Circle your response.

1. _____, those biscuits sure do smell good.

a) Mmm   b) Ew

c) Huh   d) Whee

2. _____, I stepped on an upturned nail!

a) Oops   b) Ouch

c) Shhh   d) Aw

3. _____! I left my wallet and keys on the table at the restaurant.

a) Hooray   b) Phew

c) Duh   d) Oh-no

4. _____! I knew you were the one stealing my lunch for the office refrigerator.

a) Mm-hm   b) Yum

c) A-ha   d) Blah

5. I ran away from the charging bear as I shouted, "_____! there's a bear chasing me!"

a) Run   b) Phew

c) Whee   d) Oops

6. _____, this soft drink is so incredibly refreshing.

a) Hooray   b) Ahh

c) Whew   d) Oops

7. _____! that's the fastest horse I have ever seen!

a) Um   b) Whoa

c) No   d) Boo

8. Charles put his index finger up to his lips, "_____, the people in the other room will hear you."

a) Phew   b) Shhh

c) Um   d) Hooray

9. Kim held the kitten as it softly mewed, "_____, it's so cute."

a) Mmm   b) Aw

c) Huh   d) Phew

10. Mother walked from the kitchen and asked, "_____, did any you open the extra jar of
     pickles before finishing the opened jar?"

a) Huh   b) Shhh

c) Hey   d) Oops

11. _____, we get to go to Disneyland today!

a) Huh   b) Aha

c) Yay   d) Psst

12. _____, spitting is such a nasty habit.

a) Ew   b) Aha

c) Aw   d) Er

13. _____, here comes the principal.

a) Oh   b) Um

c) Uh-oh   d) Duh

14. Principal Johnson reprimanded the student, "_____, you need to stop wasting time and get
     back to class!"

a) Yes   b) Aha

c) Hey   d) Hooray

15. _____! look at how beautiful that fireworks display is when its lighting up the sky.

a) Aha   b) Ew

c) Argh   d) Wow

16. "_____, I've had enough of this constant rain. It's been miserable for days."

a) Aw   b) Ugh

c) Huh   d) Oh

17. _____, that errant baseball just barely missed us.

a) Aw   b) Argh

c) Phew   d) Whew

18. _____, I was hoping the rain would stop in time for the county fair opening today.

a) Ooh   b) Darn

c) Ugh   d) Shhh

19. _____? I didn't catch what you were saying.

a) Aw   b) Eek

c) Huh   d) Ouch

20. _____! There's a giant wasp flying right above your head.

a) Oops   b) Look out

c) Phew   d) Argh

Chapter 7
Articles

In English, articles are words that come before a noun to indicate its specificity or generalization. There are two types of articles: definite and indefinite. These used to be called article adjectives but somewhere, somehow they got promoted to the ninth part of speech.

7.0 Articles

There are two types of articles indefinite and definite.

7.1 Indefinite Articles

Indefinite articles refer to non-specific or unidentified nouns. The two indefinite articles in English are "a" and "an." "a" is used before a singular noun that begins with a consonant sound, while "an" is used before a singular noun that begins with a vowel sound. Note: I said consonant SOUND and vowel SOUND, not the first letter of the noun that follows. Words like "hour" for example begin with a consonant but have a vowel sound, so this word "hour" gets "an" rather than "a." "I'll be there in an hour."

The word Opossum is controversial. Some pronounce it with the "O" and some do not. If you pronounce the "O" use "an" and if you pronounce it "possum" then use "a."

Examples of article usage:

A cat

An apple

A book

An umbrella

An hour (Remember: it isn't the letter the word starts with but rather the sound the word makes)

7.2 Definite Articles:

Definite articles refer to specific nouns that have already been mentioned or are easily identifiable. The definite article in English is "the."

For example:

The cat

The apple

The book

The umbrella

The hour

When to Use Articles

The use of articles depends on the context and the noun being referred to. Here are some guidelines:

Use "a" or "an" when referring to a singular, non-specific noun. For example, "I saw a dog on the street."

Use "the" when referring to a specific noun that has already been mentioned or is easily identifiable. For example, "I saw a dog on the street. The dog was brown and fluffy."

Use "the" when referring to a specific noun that is unique or one-of-a-kind. For example, "The Eiffel Tower is in Paris."

Use "a" or "an" when referring to a singular, countable noun that is part of a group. For example, "I ate an apple from the basket."

Use "the" when referring to a plural noun that is specific. For example, "I saw the cats playing in the garden."

Use no article when referring to a non-countable noun that is being used in a general sense. For example, "I like coffee." But you can use "the" with a non-countable noun like this: "Pass me the butter."

Practice Exercises:

1. Which of the following is NOT an article?

a) a

b) an

c) the

d) none of the above

2. Which article is used before a vowel sound?

a) a

b) an

c) the

d) None of the Above

3. Which article is used before a singular countable noun that is specific or particular?

a) a

b) an

c) the

d) None of the Above

4. Which article is used before a singular countable noun that is not specific or particular?

a) a

b) an

c) the

d) None of the Above

5. Which article is used before a plural countable noun that is specific or particular?

a) a

b) an

c) the

d) None of the Above

6. Which article is used before an uncountable noun?

a) a

b) an

c) the

d) none

7. Which of the following sentences uses the indefinite article correctly?

a) I need the apple

b) I need an apple

c) I need apple

d) None of the Above

8. Which of the following sentences uses the definite article correctly?

a) A cat is on the roof

b) The cat is on the roof

c) Cat is on the roof

d) None of the Above

9. Which of the following sentences uses the indefinite article correctly?

a) The book is interesting

b) A book is interesting

c) Book is interesting

d) None of the Above

10. Which of the following sentences uses the definite article correctly?

a) I saw a lion at the zoo

b) I saw lion at the zoo

c) I saw the lion at the zoo

d) None of the Above

11. Which of the following sentences uses the indefinite article correctly?

a) I am going to the school

b) I am going to a school

c) I am going to school

d) None of the Above

12. Which of the following sentences uses the definite article correctly?

a) A dog chased me yesterday

b) The dog chased me yesterday

c) Dog chased me yesterday

d) None of the Above

13. Which of the following sentences uses the indefinite article correctly?

a) He is playing the guitar

b) He is playing a guitar

c) He is playing guitar

d) None of the Above

14. Which of the following sentences uses the definite article correctly?

a) I like a pizza with extra cheese

b) I like pizza with extra cheese

c) I like the pizza with extra cheese

d) None of the Above

15. Which of the following sentences uses the indefinite article correctly?

a) I am going to the movie

b) I am going to a movie

c) I am going to movie

d) None of the Above

Articles

Directions: Read each sentence. Determine which one of your answer choices is being used as a Definite or Indefinite Article. Circle your response.

1. A number of people bought defective toasters.

a) a   b) bought

c) toasters   d) people

2. Mrs. Jenny went to the grocery store, but she forgot to buy milk.

a) buy   b) store

c) the   d) to

3. Kelly knew she couldn't eat the entire cake, yet she tried to eat it all anyway.

a) knew   b) all

c) to   d) the

4. Steven did not go to the school dance because he had a bad cold.

a) to   b) a

c) not   d) go

5. Shawn nor her husband were able to find her checkbook anywhere in the house.

a) were   b) her

c) the   d) to

6. Would you like a vanilla shake from Dairy Queen?

a) a   b) do

c) better   d) you

7. I love lemon cake, so I ate an entire half by myself.

a) it   b) myself

c) I   d) an

8. Mrs. Johnson didn't want to go to the movies, but she did anyway.

a) anyway   b) didn't

c) to   d) the

9. The astronaut opened the panel and drifted though it to the observation deck of the spacecraft.

a) of

b) the

c) and

d) it

10. There is an avalanche of work to complete spilling all over my desk.

a) there

b) it

c) an

d) was

11. An anteater would be helpful to get rid of all these ants in my garden.

a) the

b) it

c) an

d) he

12. John could neither find the puppy nor the red ball he had thrown for it to chase.

a) the

b) could

c) cure

d) nor

13. He was hoping to find the puppy or the ball beside the nearby tree.

a) he

b) tree

c) was

d) the

14. The puppy came running from the bushes for it had found the red ball.

a) for

b) the

c) from

d) had

15. The fly flew into the room and landed on the boy's head.

a) and

b) into

c) the

d) head

16. I wish I could find an excuse to take off work today.

a) an

b) excuse

c) take

d) off

17. The cowboy nor his friend knew how to fire the six shooter.

a) his

b) nor

c) friend

d) the

18. There was a reason for the giant mural of the spaceman painted on the side of the building, but no one knew what it was.

a) on   b) the

c) it   d) reason

19. Do you want tacos for dinner, or do you want a hamburger?

a) do   b) you

c) a   d) want

20. I wanted the hamburger, so mother made one for me.

a) I   b) the

c) mother   d) me

Chapter 8
Phrases and Clauses

8.0 Phrases and Clauses

Some of the parts of speech, like prepositions and conjunctions, require an understanding of phrases and clauses, so it makes sense to understand what phrases and clauses are before we look at the parts of speech that rely on them.

Phrases and clauses are important components of English grammar. They help to convey meaning and create well-structured sentences. In this chapter, we will define what phrases and clauses are, explain the different types of phrases and clauses, and provide examples of how to use them correctly. I can't stress enough how understanding the difference between a phrase and a clause is essential to many of the grammar concepts we will be visiting later in this book.

8.1 Phrases

A phrase is a group of words that function as a single unit within a sentence. The entire phrase itself can function as an adjective or adverb for example. It does not contain a **subject** and a **verb**. It can have one or the other but not both. It does not form a complete sentence on its own. Instead, a phrase functions as a noun, adjective, or adverb in a sentence. (More on this in chapters 4 and 8) There are different types of phrases:

Noun Phrase

A noun phrase functions as a noun in a sentence. It can include an article, adjective, or preposition before the noun. For example, "the red car" is a noun phrase because it functions as a single noun in a sentence. (See chapter 4 for more details)

Structure of Noun Phrases

A noun phrase typically consists of a noun, which is the head of the phrase, and one or more modifiers that provide additional information about the noun. The modifiers can include adjectives, determiners, prepositional phrases, and other nouns. For example:

The ripe **peach** on the table

A beautiful **flower** in the garden

My favorite **book** of all time

In each of these examples the head noun is in bold. The modifiers provide additional information about the noun and help to create a more detailed description.

A pre-modifier noun phrase is one that comes before the head noun in the sentence.

A post-modifier noun phrase is a noun phrase that comes after the head noun in the sentence.

Functions of Noun Phrases

Noun phrases can perform different functions in a sentence, depending on their position and context. Some common functions of noun phrases include:

Subject: A noun phrase can function as the subject of a sentence. This is called a **complete subject**. For example:

The cat chased the mouse.

<u>My sister</u> is an excellent singer.

<u>Running in the park</u> is my favorite activity.

In each of these examples, the noun phrase is the subject of the sentence and is followed by a verb.

Object: A noun phrase can function as the object of a verb. For example:

I bought <u>a new car</u>.

She gave <u>the book</u> to her friend.

They enjoyed <u>the concert</u>.

In each of these examples, the noun phrase is the object of the verb and follows it in the sentence.

Complement: A noun phrase can function as a complement in a sentence, providing additional information about the subject or object. For example:

She felt <u>like a failure.</u>

The painting is <u>a masterpiece</u>.

In each of these examples, the noun phrase is a complement and follows a linking verb such as "felt," or "is."

Noun phrases are an essential part of English grammar, providing additional information about nouns and functioning as subjects, objects, or complements in sentences. We will discuss complements in more detail in chapter 19. Go ahead and try to do the exercises for this chapter. More exercises over compliments will come later in chapter 19 as well, so you should get plenty of practice.

Adjective Phrase

An adjective phrase functions as an adjective in a sentence. It describes a noun or pronoun. For example, "the car <u>with the red paint</u>" the underlined is an adjective phrase because it describes the noun "car." (See chapter 8 for more details)

Adverbial Phrase

An adverbial phrase functions as an adverb in a sentence. It describes a verb, adjective, or another adverb. For example, "He walked <u>to the park</u>" is a sentence with an adverbial phrase "to the park." The phrase tells the reader "where" he walked. Walked is a verb and the phrase modifies it therefore it is an adverb phrase. (See chapter 8 for more details)

8.2 Clauses

A clause is a group of words that DOES contain both a subject and a verb and can form a complete sentence on its own as long as there is not a subordinating conjunction present. There are two types of clauses:

Independent Clause

An independent clause can stand alone as a sentence. It contains a subject and a verb and expresses a complete thought. For example, "She went to the store." A complete thought just means it makes sense in its entirety.

Dependent Clause

A dependent clause (sometimes called a subordinate clause) cannot stand alone as a sentence. It contains a subject and a verb but does not express a complete thought. For example, "When she went to the store." "When" is a subordinating conjunction. The clause without it would be independent and could stand alone. "She went to the store." With it, the clause is dependent on a main clause to complete the thought.

"When she went to the store" what? This clause has a subject (she) and a verb (went) but it does not make sense alone, therefore it does not have a complete thought. You need to add something to it to complete the thought. "When she went to the store, she bought milk." Now the thought is complete. What we added to the sentence for it to complete the thought is called the main clause.

"she bought milk"(a sentence with a dependent clause and a main clause to complete the thought is called a complex sentence. See chapter 13)

Types of Dependent Clauses (Yeah, allow me to overcomplicate it for you!)

Adverbial Clause

Just like an adverbial phrase, an adverbial clause functions as an adverb in a sentence. It describes a verb, adjective, or another adverb. For example, "When he arrived, I was sleeping" is a sentence with an adverbial clause "When he arrived." (Tells you when I was sleeping)

Adjectival Clause

An adjectival clause functions as an adjective in a sentence. It describes a noun or pronoun. For example, "The book I am reading is interesting" is a sentence with an adjectival clause "I am reading." (Tells you what I am reading "the book" a noun.) Yes, "interesting" is also an adjective modifying the book. It's a predicate adjective. We talk about those in chapter 17.

If this confuses you a bit, don't worry about it and just move on to the next part. When you master the parts of speech, come back here, and re-read this section. It will become completely clear to you.

Phrases and clauses are important components of English grammar. Understanding how to use them correctly can improve our ability to communicate effectively. Whether we are writing an email, a report, or a book, knowing how to use phrases and clauses can help us create clear and well-structured sentences. I'll go easy on you in the exercises.

Practice Exercises:

Identify whether the underlined portion is a phrase or a clause:

1. "<u>The man who sold me the truck</u>"

a) Phrase

b) Clause

2. Which of the following contains a dependent clause?

a) "I went to the store; I bought some milk."

b) "Because I was hungry, I went to the store."

c) "I went to the store quickly after dinner."

3. Identify the type of phrase in the following sentence:

"The girl with the red hat waved at me."

a) Prepositional phrase

b) Verb phrase

c) Adjective phrase

4. Identify whether the underlined portion is a phrase or a clause:

"<u>After I finish my homework</u>"

a) Phrase

b) Clause

5. Which of the following contains an independent clause?

a) "Although it was raining"

b) "because I went for a walk"

c) "I stayed inside."

6. Identify the opening clause in the following sentence:

"Since the store was closed, we went to the park."

a) Independent clause

b) Dependent clause

7. Identify the type of phrase in the following sentence:

"The cat in the hat chased the mouse."

a) Prepositional phrase

b) Verb phrase

c) Noun phrase

8. Identify whether the underlined portion is a phrase or a clause:

"The book that I borrowed <u>from the library</u>."

a) Phrase

b) Clause

9. Which of the following has a dependent clause?

a) "I like to eat pizza."

b) "When I get home, I will eat pizza."

c) "I ate pizza for dinner."

10. Identify the type of clause underlined in the following sentence:

"<u>Although he studied hard</u>, he failed the exam."

a) Independent clause

b) Dependent clause

Noun Phrase Exercises:

1. What is a noun phrase?

2. What is the function of a noun phrase in a sentence?

3. What is an appositive phrase in a noun phrase?

4. What is a relative clause in a noun phrase?

5. What is a post-modifier in a noun phrase?

6. What is a pre-modifier in a noun phrase?

7. What is a noun clause in a noun phrase?

8. What is a complement in a noun phrase?

9. What is a head noun in a noun phrase?

Adjective and Adverb Phrases Exercises:

1. What is an adjective phrase?

a) A group of words that modify a verb

b) A group of words that modify a noun or pronoun

c) A group of words that modify an adverb

2. What is an adverb phrase?

a) A group of words that modify a noun

b) A group of words that modify a verb, adjective, or another adverb

c) A group of words that modify a pronoun

3. Which of the following is an example of an adjective phrase?

a) The dog ran quickly

b) The car with the broken window

c) The boy spoke loudly

4. Which of the following is an example of an adverb phrase?

a) The book on the table

b) The girl with the red hair

c) The dog barked loudly

5. What is the function of an adjective phrase in a sentence?

a) To modify a verb

b) To modify a noun or pronoun

c) To modify an adverb

6. What is the function of an adverb phrase in a sentence?

a) To modify a noun

b) To modify a verb, adjective, or another adverb

c) To modify a pronoun

7. Can a prepositional phrase be used as an adjective phrase?

a) Yes

b) No

8. Can a prepositional phrase be used as an adverb phrase?

a) Yes

b) No

9. What is the difference between an adjective phrase and an adverb phrase?

a) An adjective phrase modifies a verb, while an adverb phrase modifies a noun or pronoun.

b) An adjective phrase modifies a noun or pronoun, while an adverb phrase modifies a verb, adjective, or another adverb.

c) An adjective phrase modifies a pronoun, while an adverb phrase modifies a preposition

10. Can an adverb phrase modify a noun?

a) Yes

b) No

11. Can an adjective phrase modify a verb?

a) Yes

b) No

12. Can an adjective phrase modify another adjective?

a) Yes

b) No

13. Can an adverb phrase modify a preposition?

a) Yes

b) No

14. Can an adverb phrase modify a noun clause?

a) Yes

b) No

15. Can an adverb phrase modify an entire sentence?

a) Yes

b) No

Chapter 9
Prepositions

9.0 Prepositions

Prepositions are an important part of speech that connects nouns or pronouns to other words in a sentence. They indicate the relationship between the object of the preposition and other elements of the sentence, such as the subject, verb, or another noun. In other words, they show a relationship between two nouns.

A preposition is usually placed before a noun or pronoun to form a prepositional phrase, which consists of the preposition, the object of the preposition, and any modifiers of the object. For example, in the sentence "The book is on the table," the preposition "on" connects the object "table" to the subject "book."

Or even in more simple terms, on is telling you where in space the book is located in relation to the table. It's on it.

9.1 Common Prepositions

There are many prepositions in English, but some of the most common ones include:

About, Above, Across, After, Against, Along, Among, Around, At, Before, Behind, Below, Beneath, Beside,

Between, Beyond, By, Down, During, Except, For, From, In, Inside, Into, Like, Near, Of, Off, On, Out,

Outside, Over, Past, Since, Through, Throughout, To, Toward, Under, Until, Up, Upon, With, Within,

Without.

9.2 Usage of Prepositions

Prepositions are used in a variety of ways to indicate different relationships between elements of a sentence. Some common uses of prepositions include:

Time:

Prepositions can be used to indicate the time at which something happens, such as "in," "on," "after," "during," "before," or "at." For example, "I will meet you <u>at 3 PM</u>," or "The party is <u>on Saturday</u>."

Location:

Prepositions can be used to indicate the location of something, such as "in," "on," "at," "by," or "near." For example, "The store is <u>on Main Street</u>," or "The cat is <u>under the table</u>." The prepositions are on and under and the underlined is the whole phrase. The noun at the end of the phrase is the object of the preposition.

Direction:

Prepositions can be used to indicate the direction of movement, such as "to," "from," "toward," or "away from." For example, "She walked <u>to the store</u>," or "He ran away <u>from the danger</u>."

Relationship:

Prepositions can be used to indicate a relationship between two things, such as "of," "with," or "for." For example, "The love <u>of a mother</u> <u>for her child</u> is unconditional," or "I am grateful <u>for your help</u>," "This is the sugar <u>for the cake</u>."

Comparison:

Prepositions can be used to indicate a comparison between two things, such as "like" or "than." For example, "She runs <u>like a cheetah</u>," or "He is taller <u>than his brother</u>."

It is important to use prepositions appropriately and accurately to convey the intended meaning of a sentence. Prepositions can sometimes be tricky to use correctly.

9.3 Punctuating a Prepositional Phrase:

The rule of thumb is that if a prepositional phrase appears anywhere in the sentence besides the opening phrase there is no comma; however, if the prepositional phrase **opens** a sentence and it is longer than **three** words or if there are two phrases together there should be a comma after the phrase or phrases. For Example:

At the end of a long day, I like to relax. "At the end" and "of a long day" are two prepositional phrases together. Put a comma after the second one.

"Over the Rocky Mountains, we traveled." The opening prepositional phrase has more than three words, so a comma is placed after mountains. "Over the mountains we traveled." would not have a comma because the opening prepositional phrase is only three words.

After the rain the air smelled fresh. After the rain is a phrase only three words long so no comma is needed.

Prepositions, specifically ending a sentence with a preposition is another one of those controversial topics in English grammar. When I am writing (except in dialogue where anything goes) I try not to end a sentence with a preposition. When speaking I don't even think about it. If you overhear an argument, you might say to your friend standing next to you: "What was all that about?" "About" is a preposition, and I don't see anything wrong with ending that particular sentence with it. I would say avoid ending sentences with a preposition in writing especially academic writing just to be safe.

Pre-Quiz Practice Exercises:

1. **Prepositions:**

1. I will meet you _____ the library.

A.) at

B.) on

C.) in

D.) under

2. The ball is _____ the box.

A.) over

B.) beside

C.) in

D.) between

3. She was sitting _____ the couch.

A.) at

B.) on

C.) in

D.) above

4. The cat is sleeping _____ the chair.

A.) under

B.) beside

C.) on

D.) between

5. We will arrive _____ the airport at 8 PM.

A.) on

B.) in

C.) at

D.) under

6. The school is _____ the hospital and the park.

A.) between

B.) over

C.) under

D.) through

7. The vase is _____ the table.

A.) beside

B.) on

C.) under

D.) between

8. The keys are _____ the drawer.

A.) in

B.) on

C.) above

D.) behind

9. She lives _____ her parents.

A.) with

B.) in

C.) on

D.) under

10. The dog is hiding _____ the bed.

A.) in

B.) on

C.) over

D.) beside

1. **Prepositions and Antecedents:**

1. Which of the following is an example of a preposition?

A.) dog

B.) under

C.) happy

D.) car

2. Which of the following is the correct use of a preposition?

A.) They went to the movies with she.

B.) He gave the gift to him and I.

C.) She stood beside her friend.

D.) The dog chased the ball in him.

3. Which of the following is the antecedent of this sentence? The cat cleaned its tail.

A.) cat

B.) tail

C.) cleaned

D.) its

4. Which of the following is a correct use of an antecedent?

A.) He said that they would meet at the park, but it was too hot.

B.) She gave her friend the bracelet, and she loved it.

C.) The car needed new tires, so it went to the mechanic.

D.) The students were told they had a test the next day.

5. Which of the following is a preposition that can indicate location?

A.) between

B.) for

C.) until

D.) above

6. Which of the following is an example of a correct pronoun-antecedent agreement?

A.) Everyone forgot their books at home.

B.) Students should bring his or her own calculator.

C.) The team celebrated its victory with a pizza party.

D.) The employees requested their paychecks be delivered early.

7. Which of the following is a correct use of a pronoun-antecedent agreement?

A.) Neither the dog nor the cat would eat their food.

B.) Either my sister or my brother will bring their car.

C.) Everyone in the room should raise their hand.

D.) The children didn't want to do their homework.

8. Which of the following is an antecedent that refers to a person?

A.) The book

B.) The car

C.) The dog

D.) The teacher

9. Which of the following is the correct use of a preposition to show movement?

A.) She jumped in the bed.

B.) He walked on the street.

C.) They swam above the water.

D.) The bird flew between the trees.

Prepositions Worksheet

Part One | Identifying Prepositions

Directions: Read each sentence. Determine which one of your answer choices is being used as a preposition. Circle your response.

1. The math student was horrified to realize she had left her calculator at home.

a) her
b) home
c) to
d) at

2. The superhero movie played after the main feature.

a) after
b) played
c) the
d) main

3. Jill wanted to eat the cupcakes with the colorful sprinkles.

a) colorful
b) with
c) the
d) to

4. Jonathan had collected coins for many years, so he knew their value.

a) he
b) all
c) had
d) for

5. Lexi thought the rice might be stored in the pantry.

a) the
b) in
c) thought
d) rice

6. Roger Sanderson, a teacher, was tired of his students' bad behavior.

a) of
b) bad
c) was
d) a

7. The stuntman drove the stunt car through the burning hoop.

a) drove
b) hoop
c) burning
d) through

8. The farmers are always worried about their crops until the first rain.

a) about
b) the

c) until   d) both a & c

9. The cowboy fought the bear and against all odds he won.

a) and   b) against

c) he   d) odds

10. The old man was without a doubt the meanest man who ever lived.

a) without   b) who

c) meanest   d) ever

11. Jacob found his new kitten hiding under the bed.

a) his   b) bed

c) under   d) hiding

12. Susie was thankful she finished all her homework before dinner.

a) dinner   b) she

c) her   d) before

13. The kids took turns jumping over the water sprinkler.

a) over   b) water

c) the   d) took

14. Before it snows many people rush to the grocery store to prepare for the storm.

a) before   b) to

c) for   d) all the above

15. Before you can go outside during a snowstorm you must bundle up first.

a) before   b) during

c) you   d) bundle

16. Nothing is sacred between two lovers.

a) is   b) two

c) between   d) nothing

17. The fight took place near the stage and moved toward the crowd.

a) the   b) crowd

c) toward   d) fight

18. The hot kids jumped into the cool water of the swimming pool.

a) hot

b) of

c) into

d) Both b & c

19. Dennis chose a donut from the many that lined the colorful shelves.

a) from

b) lined

c) the

d) a

20. The character Indiana Jones has a notorious fear of snakes.

a) has

b) of

c) fear

d) snakes

21. Because it was underpowered, the car barely made it over the hill.

a) made

b) it

c) car

d) over

22. Running as fast as he could, John ran into the burning building to save the children.

a) as

b) to

c) into

d) the

23. People waited outside the movie theatre for hours waiting to get tickets.

a) outside

b) hours

c) waited

d) to

24. The bank robber tried to escape but the police officer caught him at the door.

a) tried

b) but

c) at

d) the

Part Two | Redundant Prepositions

Directions: Read each sentence. Determine which one of your answer choices is a redundant or unnecessary preposition. Circle your response.

25. The boy threw the banana peel out of the window of the tree house after he finished eating his lunch.

a) the

b) out

c) after

d) of

26. The eager boy located where the coins were at, and he put them into his coin collection.

a)   where   b)   at

c)   his   d)   into

27.   The children ran outside of the house determined to play in the water sprinkler.

a)   in   b)   outside

c)   the   d)   of

28.   The old man looked around for his daughter wondering where she went to after supper.

a)   for   b)   looked

c)   to   d)   went

29.   The rock star jumped off of the stage, landed safely in the arms of his fans, was carried above
      their heads, and then put back on the stage.

a)   in   b)   above

c)   of   d)   off

30.   The man addressed the boy playing in his front yard, "Where's your dad at?"

a)   the   b)   at

c)   in   d)   his

Chapter 10
Conjunctions

Conjunctions are an important part of speech that connect words, phrases, or clauses within a sentence. They help to clarify the relationships between different parts of a sentence and to make our writing more coherent and cohesive. The Latin root word "junct" literally means join.

10.0 Types of Conjunctions

There are three main types of conjunctions: coordinating conjunctions, subordinating conjunctions, and correlative conjunctions.

10.1 Coordinating Conjunctions:

Coordinating conjunctions connect two independent clauses, or two equal sentence elements. They are used to join two ideas of equal importance, and include the following:

For

And

Nor

But

Or

Yet

So

If you notice the bolded letters, you can remember all seven coordinating conjunctions easily as FANBOYS.

Two independent clauses connected by a coordinating conjunction is called a compound sentence.

For example: "She wanted to go to the store, but it was raining outside." She wanted to go to the store. Is an independent clause, and It was raining outside. is an independent clause.

You could also join these two sentences with a semicolon. She wanted to go to the store: it was raining outside. You just can't combine them with a comma because that would be a comma splice. Commas cannot be used to combine two independent clauses.

10.2 Subordinating Conjunctions:

Subordinating conjunctions connect an independent clause with a dependent clause (sometimes called a subordinate clause), or a sentence element that cannot stand alone as a complete sentence. They indicate a relationship of dependence between the two clauses and include the following:

After, Although, As, Because, Before, Even though, If, Since, That, Unless, Until, When, Where, While

For example: "I will go for a walk <u>after I finish my work</u>."

But wait a second! In the last chapter on prepositions, I told you after, before, since, and other words were prepositions. How can they now be subordinating conjunctions? Simple, if they are used with a phrase, they are prepositions: after it rains, before it snows, since yesterday, until noon. Etc. If they are used with a clause, they are subordinate conjunctions: After you go the store, before you arrived, since you asked, until I failed. Remember a clause has both a subject and a verb: You go, you arrived, you asked, I failed. Etc.

10.3 Correlative Conjunctions:

Correlative Conjunctions: Correlative conjunctions are used in pairs to connect two equal sentence elements, such as nouns, verbs, or adjectives. They include the following pairs:

Both/and

Either/or

Neither/nor

Not only/but also

Whether/or

For example: "She is not only smart but also kind."

We tend to not pay much attention to these conjunctions. Just remember they come in pairs.

10.4 Usage of Conjunctions

Conjunctions are used to join words, phrases, and clauses within a sentence, and to show the relationship between them. They can be used in a variety of ways, including:

Coordinating Conjunctions:

Coordinating conjunctions are used to join two independent clauses or two equal sentence elements. They can also be used to join words, phrases, or clauses of the same type.

Subordinating Conjunctions:

Subordinating conjunctions are used to join an independent clause with a dependent clause. They can indicate the cause, effect, time, or condition of the action in the dependent clause. They do not join words or phrases, just clauses. Independent clauses joined together with dependent clauses with a subordinating conjunction are called complex sentences.

Correlative Conjunctions:

Correlative conjunctions are used to join two equal sentence elements, such as nouns, verbs, or adjectives. They are always used in pairs and are placed before each sentence element.

Conjunctions don't have to be difficult. With a little practice, they are easy to master.

Pre-Quiz Practice Exercises:

Coordinating Conjunctions:

1. Which of the following is a coordinating conjunction?

a) because

b) although

c) and

d) since

2. Which coordinating conjunction is used to express a contrast or opposition?

a) and

b) but

c) or

d) so

3. Which coordinating conjunction is used to express a choice between two options?

a) and

b) but

c) or

d) so

4. Which coordinating conjunction is used to express a reason or cause?

a) and

b) but

c) or

d) for

5. Which coordinating conjunction is used to express a result or consequence?

a) and

b) but

c) or

d) so

6. Which coordinating conjunction is used to express a condition?

a) and

b) but

c) or

d) if

7. Which coordinating conjunction is used to express a continuation or addition?

a) and

b) but

c) or

d) so

8. Which coordinating conjunction is used to express a comparison?

a) and

b) but

c) or

d) as

9. Which coordinating conjunction is used to express a concession or contrast?

a) and

b) but

c) or

d) yet

10. Which coordinating conjunction is used to express a purpose?

a) and

b) but

c) or

d) for

Subordinating Conjunctions:

1. Which of the following is a subordinating conjunction?

A) and

B) because

C) nor

D) both A and C

2. What does a subordinating conjunction do in a sentence?

A) connects two independent clauses

B) introduces a dependent clause

C) adds emphasis to a sentence

D) none of the above

3. Which of the following is a subordinating conjunction that shows time?

A) although

B) since

C) before

D) but

4. Which of the following is a subordinating conjunction that shows contrast?

A) however

B) because

C) yet

D) both A and C

5. Which subordinating conjunction is used to show cause and effect?

A) although

B) unless

C) therefore

D) neither A nor B

6. Which subordinating conjunction is used to show purpose?

A) since

B) in order that

C) even though

D) both A and C

7. Which subordinating conjunction is used to show condition?

A) unless

B) although

C) both A and B

D) neither A nor B

8. Which of the following sentences uses a subordinating conjunction correctly?

A) I will go to the store, and I will buy some milk.

B) Because it was raining, we decided to cancel the picnic.

C) She ate dinner, she watched a movie.

D) None of the above

9. Which of the following subordinating conjunctions shows a comparison?

A) as

B) since

C) unless

D) both B and C

10. Which of the following sentences uses a subordinating conjunction incorrectly?

A) Although he was sick, he still went to work.

B) I will go to the store after I finish my homework.

C) Because she was hungry, she decided to take a nap.

D) All of the Above

Correlative Conjunctions:

1. What are correlative conjunctions?

A) They are conjunctions that connect two independent clauses

B) They are conjunctions that connect a dependent clause to an independent clause

C) They are pairs of conjunctions that work together to connect sentence elements

D) None of the above

2. Which of the following is a correlative conjunction?

A) and

B) because

C) either...or

D) both A and B

3. What is the purpose of using correlative conjunctions?

A) To add emphasis to a sentence

B) To connect two independent clauses

C) To show cause and effect

D) To connect two sentence elements that have equal importance

4. Which of the following correlative conjunctions is used to show a contrast?

A) neither...nor

B) both...and

C) either...or

D) not only...but also

5. Which of the following sentences uses a correlative conjunction correctly?

A) Either you come with me, or I will go alone.

B) Not only I like pizza, but my sister likes it too.

C) Neither my mom nor my dad can speak French.

D) Both A and C

Coordinating Conjunctions

Directions: Read each sentence. Determine which one of your answer choices is being used as a coordinating conjunction. Circle your response.

1. Jason and Nicole found a box of coins buried in their back yard.

a) a

b) found

c) coins

d) and

2. Mrs. Jenny went to the grocery store, but she forgot to buy milk.

a) buy

b) the

c) but

d) to

3. Kelly knew she couldn't eat the entire cake, yet she tried to eat it all anyway.

a) knew

b) all

c) to

d) yet

4. Steven did not go to the school dance for he had nothing formal to wear.

a) to

b) for

c) not

d) go

5. Shawn nor her husband were able to find her checkbook.

a) were

b) her

c) nor

d) to

6. Do you like Dairy Queen's burger or do you like Sonic's burger better?

a) or

b) do

c) better

d) you

7. I love lemon cake, so I ate half of it myself.

a) it

b) myself

c) I

d) so

8. Mrs. Johnson didn't want to go to the movies, but she did anyway.

a) anyway

b) didn't

c) to

d) but

9. The astronaut opened the panel and drifted though it to the observation deck of the spacecraft.

a) of   b) and

c) the   d) it

10. The principal wanted to cancel the game due to snow, yet he knew how important it was for the game to continue.

a) the   b) it

c) yet   d) was

11. The superhero was afraid to get caught up in his cape, so he got rid of it.

a) the   b) it

c) so   d) he

12. John could neither find the puppy nor the red ball he had thrown for it to chase.

a) nor   b) could

c) cure   d) the

13. He was hoping to find the puppy or the ball beside the nearby tree.

a) he   b) tree

c) the   d) or

14. The puppy came running from the bushes for it had found the red ball.

a) the   b) for

c) from   d) had

15. The fly flew into the room and landed on the boy's head.

a) the   b) into

c) and   d) head

16. I cannot risk any more of my money gambling, for if I do, I will be broke.

a) for   b) do

c) broke   d) of

17. The cowboy nor his friend knew how to fire the six shooter.

a) his   b) the

c) friend   d) nor

18. There was a reason for the giant mural of the spaceman painted on the side of the building, but no one knew what it was.

a) on   b) but

c) it   d) reason

19.   Do you want tacos for dinner, or do you want hamburgers?

a) do   b) you

c) or   d) want

20.   I wanted tacos so mother made them for me.

a) I   b) so

c) mother   d) me

Subordinating Conjunctions Worksheet

Directions: Read each sentence. Determine which one of your answer choices is used as a subordinating conjunction. Circle your response.

1. The boy could run circles around his grandfather if he decided he wanted to prove himself.

a) if
b) he
c) decided
d) to

2. While participating in the event, Tabitha ran faster than any of the other girls.

a) ran
b) faster
c) of
d) while

3. When the storm started, the townsfolk were prepared for it.

a) were
b) it
c) when
d) started

4. Gene wore a yellow raincoat even though the forecast didn't call for rain.

a) wore
b) even though
c) forecast
d) call for

5. Juan decided to drive his truck all night since he was due to pick another load early in the morning.

a) in the
b) of
c) since
d) to pick

6. When the spring storm blew in, the high winds knocked down power lines and toppled trees.

a) When
b) high
c) spring
d) and

7. Once the evil queen was thwarted, the kingdom finally felt safe enough for the subjects to return.

a) for
b) kingdom
c) evil
d) once

8. Roy has played the guitar since he was a young boy.

a) and
b) since
c) has
d) was

9. Jason and his brother both practiced their guitars until they each had calloused fingers.

a) in

b) until

c) each

d) his

10. Gene almost stepped on the rattlesnake even though he was being very careful.

a) almost stepped

b) he was

c) even though

d) very careful

11. Unless they found shelter from the storm, the boys were going to get pelted by the rain.

a) by

b) were

c) they

d) unless

12. After all the food was eaten, the staff gathered up the dishes for washing.

a) After

b) was eaten

c) staff

d) for

13. The party goers laughed as the court jester sang and danced.

a) the

b) and

c) as

d) court

14. The soldiers were trapped behind enemy lines until the others in their platoon mounted a rescue.

a) were trapped

b) in their

c) soldiers

d) until

15. Jason stepped aside so that his brother bill could have a turn at the dart game.

a) so

b) brother

c) so that

d) a

16. Whenever I think of my childhood, I think about how lucky I was to have such great parents.

a) about

b) whenever

c) lucky

d) to have

17. Mother preferred the strong arm approach whereas father often let things slide.

a) whereas

b) approach

c) let

d) often

18. Because all the cake was gone, John cut himself a big piece of pie instead.

a) all

b) was

c) because

d) of

19. Although the mountain was steep, Keith didn't give up until he had reached the top.

a) although

b) until

c) steep

d) both a & b

20. Even though Beth studied the material for hours, she still just barely passed the exams.

a) just

b) barely

c) studied

d) even though

Cumulative Quiz 1 Answers

1. A
2. C
3. D
4. B
5. C
6. A
7. B
8. C
9. D
10. C
11. C
12. A
13. D
14. B
15. A
16. C
17. A
18. D
19. D
20. B
21. A
22. B
23. A
24. D
25. A
26. C
27. B
28. A
29. C
30. A
31. A
32. C
33. B
34. D

35. C
36. B
37. C
38. D
39. B
40. C

16. Hey! You are running the wrong way.

a) you

b) running

c) hey

d) way

17. Oh no, I forgot to buy the tickets for the concert!

a) oh no

b) concert

c) forgot

d) buy

18. Finally! That receiver did his job and caught the ball!

a) caught

b) receiver

c) did his

d) finally

Identify the Noun(s)

19. Georgia Dennings is finally running for president.

a) Georgia Dennings

b) finally

c) president

d) both a & c

20. That is one beautiful car.

a) that

b) car

c) beautiful

d) all of the above

21. John wanted to go.

a) John

b) go

c) wanted

d) both a & c

Identify the Pronouns(s)

22. You are a good friend, Harry.

a) friend

b) you

c) are

d) harry

23. I wanted to travel across the river on a ferry rather than a bridge.

a) I

b) river

c) ferry

d) bridge

24. Jill wanted cookies so mother made chocolate chip cookies for her.

a) cookies

b) so

c) mother

d) her

Identify the Preposition(s)

25. Do you want fries with your hamburger?

a) with

b) you

c) fries

d) want

26. Please tell you made the reservation like I asked.

a) you

b) like

c) both a & d

d) I

27. Would you call the family inside for me?

a) you

b) both a & d

c) family

d) me

Identify the Verbs(s)

28. Run as fast as you can to the neighbor's house.

a) run

b) you can

c) fast

d) as

29. Jason cried when Old Yeller died.

a) Jason

b) when

c) cried

d) died

30. Fred Johnson is the new janitor who will be here later today.

a) is

b) new

c) the

d) who

What type of Verb is bolded in the following sentences?

31. We will **have to** stop by the store on the way home.

a) modal

b) stative

c) phrasal

d) action

32. You had better **wake up** early tomorrow, so we can leave on time.

a) modal

b) stative

c) phrasal   d) linking

33.   Have you been **seeing** John on the side?

a) modal   b) stative

c) phrasal   d) to be

34.   I will **be seeing** the band for the first time this Tuesday!

a) modal   b) stative

c) phrasal   d) verb phrase

35.   If your friends told you to go **jump off** a bridge, would you do that too?

a) modal   b) stative

c) phrasal   d) action

What is the Denominal Adjective in the following sentences?

36.   Did you find your tennis shoes?

a) shoes   b) tennis

c) you   d) your

37.   How many times did you have to take your chemistry exam?

a) you   b) exam

c) chemistry   d) take

38.   I need to find a good camper trailer to take on the trip with us.

a) I   b) trailer

c) trip   d) camper

39.   That is a famous suspension bridge up ahead.

a) famous   b) suspension

c) that   d) bridge

40.   Put down that cigarette lighter.

a) you   b) put

c) cigarette   d) lighter

Chapter 11
The Twelve Verb Tenses

11.0 12 Verb Tenses

Verbs are an essential part of every sentence. They indicate actions, events, or states of being. There are twelve verb tenses in the English language, and each of them has a specific purpose. Here we go with taking past, present, and future tenses and overcomplicating them! You're welcome! For this workbook I'm not going to go too deep into this. I just want you to know what they are and that they exist.

11.1 Present Simple Tense

The present simple tense is used to describe actions that occur regularly or habits. It is also used to state facts or general truths. The present simple tense uses the base form of the verb.

Example: I play tennis every Monday.

11.2 Present Continuous Tense

The present continuous tense is used to describe actions that are currently happening or ongoing. It is formed by using the present tense of the verb 'to be' with the present participle form of the main verb. Continuous tense verbs always end in -ing.

Example: She is reading a book right now.

11.3 Present Perfect Tense

The present perfect tense is used to describe actions that occurred at an unspecified time in the past and have a connection to the present. It is formed by using the present tense of the verb 'to have' with the past participle form of the main verb. Most of the time perfect tense verbs end in -ed.

Example: I have lived in New York for five years.

11.4 Present Perfect Continuous Tense

The present perfect continuous tense is used to describe actions that started in the past and are still ongoing or have just stopped. It is formed by using the present tense of the verb 'to have' with 'been' and the present participle form of the main verb.

Example: They have been playing football for two hours.

11.5 Past Simple Tense

The past simple tense is used to describe actions that occurred at a specific time in the past. It is formed by using the past form of the main verb.

Example: She walked to the store yesterday.

11.6 Past Continuous Tense

The past continuous tense is used to describe actions that were ongoing at a specific time in the past. It is formed by using the past tense of the verb 'to be' with the present participle form of the main verb.

Example: I was eating dinner when she called.

11.7 Past Perfect Tense

The past perfect tense is used to describe actions that occurred before a specific time in the past. It is formed by using the past tense of the verb 'to have' with the past participle form of the main verb.

Example: They had finished their homework before they went to bed.

11.8 Past Perfect Continuous Tense

The past perfect continuous tense is used to describe actions that had been ongoing for a period of time before a specific time in the past. It is formed by using the past tense of the verb 'to have' with 'been' and the present participle form of the main verb.

Example: I had been studying for hours before the exam.

11.9 Future Simple Tense

The future simple tense is used to describe actions that will occur in the future. It is formed by using the base form of the verb with 'will'.

Example: He will visit his grandparents next week.

11.10 Future Continuous Tense

The future continuous tense is used to describe actions that will be ongoing at a specific time in the future. It is formed by using the future tense of the verb 'to be' with the present participle form of the main verb. "Will" is still used and will always be used to indicate future tense in all its forms.

Example: I will be watching TV at eight o'clock tonight.

11.11 Future Perfect Tense

The future perfect tense is used to describe actions that will have been completed at a specific time in the future. It is formed by using the future tense of the verb 'to have' with the past participle form of the main verb.

Example: By next year, he will have graduated from college.

11.12 Future Perfect Continuous Tense

The future perfect continuous tense is a verb tense that is used to describe an ongoing action that will be completed at a specific time in the future. It is formed by using the auxiliary verb "will" or "shall" with "have been" and the present participle form of the main verb.

Example: By next year, I will have been studying for ten years.

In this example, the action of studying will have been ongoing for ten years by the time next year comes around. The future perfect continuous tense is used to emphasize the duration of an ongoing action up until a specific point in the future. It is commonly used to talk about actions that started in the past and are expected to continue into the future.

Example: By the time she retires, she will have been teaching for thirty years.

In this example, the action of teaching started in the past and is expected to continue up until the point when the speaker is referring to, which is the time when the woman retires. The future perfect continuous tense is often used in formal writing, such as academic or technical documents, to describe ongoing processes or activities that are expected to continue into the future.

Exercises:

1. Which tense is used to describe an action that will happen in the future?

a) Present Perfect

b) Future Simple

c) Past Continuous

d) Present Continuous

2. Which tense is used to describe an action that started in the past and continues up to the present?

a) Past Simple

b) Present Continuous

c) Present Perfect Continuous

d) Present Perfect

3. Which tense is used to describe an action that was completed at a specific time in the past?

a) Present Perfect

b) Past Continuous

c) Past Simple

d) Future Simple

4. Which tense is used to describe an action that started and finished in the past?

a) Present Perfect Continuous

b) Past Simple

c) Past Perfect

d) Future Simple

5. Which tense is used to describe an action that will be ongoing at a future time?

a) Present Continuous

b) Future Continuous

c) Past Perfect Continuous

d) Present Perfect Continuous

6. Which tense is used to describe an action that happened before another action in the past?

a) Past Simple

b) Past Perfect

c) Future Simple

d) Present Perfect

7. Which tense is used to describe an action that is happening right now?

a) Present Perfect Continuous

b) Present Continuous

c) Past Continuous

d) Past Perfect Continuous

8. Which tense is used to describe an action that will have been completed by a certain time in the future?

a) Present Perfect

b) Past Simple

c) Future Perfect

d) Past Perfect Continuous

9. Which tense is used to describe an action that had been completed before another action in the past?

a) Present Perfect Continuous

b) Past Perfect

c) Future Simple

d) Present Simple

10. Which tense is used to describe an action that will have been ongoing for a certain amount of time by a future time?

a) Present Continuous

b) Future Perfect Continuous

c) Past Simple

d) Past Perfect Continuous

11. Which tense is used to describe an action that is expected to happen in the near future?

a) Future Simple

b) Present Perfect

c) Past Continuous

d) Present Simple

12. Which tense is used to describe an action that is habitually done in the past?

a) Past Simple

b) Past Continuous

c) Past Perfect

d) Past Perfect Continuous

13. Which tense is used to describe an action that was ongoing in the past but was interrupted by another action?

a) Present Perfect Continuous

b) Past Perfect Continuous

c) Past Continuous

d) Present Continuous

14. Which tense is used to describe an action that had been completed before a specific time in the past?

a) Past Perfect

b) Present Perfect

c) Future Simple

d) Present Simple

15. Which tense is used to describe an action that will be completed at a specific time in the future?

a) Present Perfect

b) Future Simple

c) Past Simple

d) Present Simple

Part 2

Sentence Structure and Mechanics

Chapter 12
Sentence Types

12.1 THE 4 SENTENCE TYPES

In this chapter, we will discuss the four main types of sentences: declarative, interrogative, imperative, and exclamatory. Each type of sentence has its own unique purpose and structure.

Declarative Sentences

A declarative sentence is a statement that declares or asserts a fact or idea. It ends with a period. For example:

The grass is green.

The cat yowls at night.

I love white chocolate.

Declarative sentences are the most common type of sentence in written and spoken English. They are used to convey information or opinions. In English we usually write a declarative sentence like this: subject+verb. When a sentence is rarely written verb+subject (Learn you will.) We call that a Yoda...er... I mean an inverted sentence. The dad jokes just keep coming, sorry!

Interrogative Sentences

An interrogative sentence is a sentence that asks a question. It ends with a question mark. For example:

Are you coming to the party tonight?

What time does the movie start?

How do I get to the bus station?

When you watch a movie and the bad cop is interrogating the perp, he is asking the suspect questions. Interrogate has the same root word as interrogative. Interrogate=interrogative. It means you are asking questions.

Interrogative sentences are used to seek information or clarification. They often begin with a question word such as "who," "what," "when," "where," "why," or "how."

Imperative Sentences

An imperative sentence is a sentence that gives a command, direction, or instruction. It ends with a period or an exclamation point. This sentence has no written subject because the subject is understood to be "you" For example:

Close the door, please. ("You" close the door, please.)

Turn off the lights before you leave. ("You" turn off the lights before you leave.)

Be quiet in the library. ("You" be quiet in the library.)

Again, Imperative sentences are used to issue orders or instructions. They often begin with a verb in its base form, and the subject is implied "you".

Exclamatory Sentences

An exclamatory sentence is a sentence that expresses strong emotion or excitement. It ends with an exclamation point. For example:

What a wonderful time we had shopping today!

I can't believe we won the game!

Wow, that's incredible!

Exclamatory sentences are used to convey strong feelings such as joy, surprise, or anger. They are called exclamatory because someone is exclaiming an emotion and they end with an exclamation point.

So, that wasn't so bad. There are easy ways to remember the sentence types. Declare something = declarative, interrogate someone = ask questions = interrogative, give a command or issue an imperative = imperative (also doesn't have a written subject in the sentence), and finally exclaim an emotion and end with an exclamation point = exclamatory.

Once again, understanding the different types of sentences is essential for effective communication in written and spoken English. Declarative sentences state facts or ideas, interrogative sentences ask questions, imperative sentences give commands or instructions, and exclamatory sentences express strong emotions. By using the appropriate sentence type, we can convey our intended meaning and engage our audience.

Sentence structure is the arrangement of words, phrases, and clauses to create meaningful sentences. In English, a basic sentence consists of a subject, a verb, and an object usually in that order. However, sentence structure can be more complex, depending on the type of sentence being used.

12.2 TYPES OF SENTENCE STRUCTURE

Simple Sentences

A simple sentence is a sentence that consists of a single independent clause. An independent clause contains a subject and a predicate. It can stand alone as a complete sentence. Simple means they are not complicated. Sible sentences can contain compound subjects and predicates and still be simple. For example:

The German shepherd and Doberman pinscher barked. (compound subject)

She hums and sings beautifully. (compound predicate or compound verb if you wish)

The sun rises in the east.

Compound Sentences

A compound sentence consists of two or more independent clauses that are joined by a **coordinating** conjunction, such as "and," "but," or "or." If you remove the conjunction, you have two simple sentences. You can also join two independent clauses with a semicolon. For example:

I like to read books, but my sister prefers to watch movies.

The sky was blue, and the sun was shining. With semicolon: The sky was blue; the sun was shining.

He went to the store, and she stayed home.

Complex Sentences

A complex sentence consists of one independent clause and at least one dependent (subordinate) clause, which cannot stand alone as a complete sentence. Dependent clauses begin with subordinating conjunctions, such as "because," "although," or "since." For example:

Although it was raining, we decided to go for a walk.

Because I was tired, I went to bed early. (comma after dependent clause) Also: I went to bed early because I was tired. (no comma)

Since she missed the bus, she had to walk to school. (comma after dependent clause) Also: She had to walk to school since she missed the bus. (no comma)

Punctuation Note:

The comma after the opening dependent clause is only used when the dependent clause is the first clause in the sentence. If the dependent clause comes second, no comma is needed. See the example in the second and third sentences above.

Compound-Complex Sentences

A compound-complex sentence consists of two or more independent clauses and at least one dependent clause. This type of sentence combines the features of compound and complex sentences. For example:

She wanted to go to the beach, but it was too cold, so she stayed home.

12.3 NOT A SENTENCE

Sentence Fragment

A sentence fragment is just what it sounds like. It is a part of a sentence. Sentence fragments are used sometimes in dialogue because people rarely speak in complete sentences. In order to have a complete sentence, you need three things: a subject, a verb, and a complete thought. (It has to make logical sense. Remember subordinating conjunctions?) IN dialogue you might have something like;

"Hey, Diane, you want to get a burger?"

Sure."

"All right, where?"

These are fragments. Here is what it would look like if done in complete sentences;

"Hey, Diane, would you like to go and get a burger with me?"

"Sure, I would like that."

"All right, where would you like to go?"

Outside of dialogue I can't think of any other place to use a sentence fragment effectively. There may be another way to use them but I can't think of any. They are usually considered bad writing.

Runon Sentences

These are sentences where the full stop period or other end mark is omittted and the sentences just run on like they just keep going even though they could be split up into many sentences with end marks or commas but there is nothing to stop it. See what I did there?

Practice Exercises:

1. Identify the sentence type of the following sentence: "The cat sat on the mat."

a) Declarative

b) Interrogative

c) Imperative

d) Exclamatory

2. Which sentence type is used to make a request or give a command?

a) Declarative

b) Interrogative

c) Imperative

d) Exclamatory

3. Which sentence type ends with a period?

a) Declarative

b) Interrogative

c) Imperative

d) Exclamatory

4. Which sentence type is used to express strong emotions or feelings?

a) Declarative

b) Interrogative

c) Imperative

d) Exclamatory

5. Identify the sentence type of the following sentence: "What time is it?"

a) Declarative

b) Interrogative

c) Imperative

d) Exclamatory

6. Which sentence type is used to ask a question?

a) Declarative

b) Interrogative

c) Imperative

d) Exclamatory

7. Identify the sentence type of the following sentence: "Don't forget your keys."

a) Declarative

b) Interrogative

c) Imperative

d) Exclamatory

8. Which sentence type is used to give a piece of information or make a statement?

a) Declarative

b) Interrogative

c) Imperative

d) Exclamatory

9. Identify the sentence type of the following sentence: "I can't believe it!"

a) Declarative

b) Interrogative

c) Imperative

d) Exclamatory

10. Which sentence type is used to express surprise, anger, or other intense emotions?

a) Declarative

b) Interrogative

c) Imperative

d) Exclamatory

11. Identify the sentence type of the following sentence: "Please pass me the salt and pepper."

a) Declarative

b) Interrogative

c) Imperative

d) Exclamatory

12. Which sentence type is used to express a strong desire or hope?

a) Declarative

b) Interrogative

c) Imperative

d) Exclamatory

13. Identify the sentence type of the following sentence: "The sun is shining brightly."

a) Declarative

b) Interrogative

c) Imperative

d) Exclamatory

14. Which sentence type is used to make a statement or give information?

a) Declarative

b) Interrogative

c) Imperative

d) Exclamatory

15. Identify the sentence type of the following sentence: "How are you feeling today?"

a) Declarative

b) Interrogative

c) Imperative

d) Exclamatory

Sentence Structure Exercises:

1. What is a sentence?

a) A group of letters

b) A group of words that expresses a complete thought and contains a subject and a predicate

c) A paragraph

2. Which part of a sentence performs the action or is the focus of the sentence?

a) Predicate

b) Object

c) Subject

3. Which part of a sentence tells what the subject does or what is done to the subject?

a) Predicate

b) Object

c) Subject

4. What is a simple sentence?

a) A sentence that contains one independent clause and expresses a complete thought

b) A sentence that contains two or more independent clauses joined by a conjunction or semicolon

c) A sentence that contains one dependent clause

5. What is a compound sentence?

a) A sentence that contains one independent clause and one or more dependent clauses

b) A sentence that contains two or more independent clauses joined by a conjunction or semicolon

c) A group of words that does not express a complete thought

6. What is a dependent clause?

a) A group of words that contains a subject and a verb but cannot stand alone as a complete sentence

b) A sentence that contains one independent clause and one or more dependent clauses

c) A group of words that does not express a complete thought

7. What is a run-on sentence?

a) A sentence in which two or more independent clauses are improperly joined

b) A sentence that contains one independent clause and one or more dependent clauses

c) A group of words that does not express a complete thought

8. What is a fragment sentence?

a) A sentence in which two or more independent clauses are improperly joined

b) A group of words that does not express a complete thought and cannot stand alone as a sentence

c) A sentence that contains one dependent clause

9. What is a misplaced modifier?

a) A word or phrase that is in the wrong place in a sentence and creates confusion or ambiguity

b) A sentence in which two or more independent clauses are improperly joined

c) A sentence that contains one independent clause and one or more dependent clauses

10. What is a comma splice?

a) A sentence in which two or more independent clauses are improperly joined with a comma

b) A sentence that contains one dependent clause

c) A group of words that does not express a complete thought and cannot stand alone as a sentence

Sentence Types

Directions: Read each sentence. Determine if the sentence is a Declarative, Interrogative, Imperative, or Exclamatory sentence. Circle your response.

1. Jason and Nicole found a box of coins buried in their back yard.

a) Exclamatory   b) Imperative

c) Interrogative   d) Declarative

2. Mrs. Jenny went to the grocery store, but she forgot to buy milk.

a) Exclamatory   b) Imperative

c) Interrogative   d) Declarative

3. Kelly knew she couldn't eat the entire cake, yet she tried to eat it all anyway.

a) Exclamatory   b) Imperative

c) Interrogative   d) Declarative

4. Where did you get that new car?

a) Exclamatory   b) Imperative

c) Interrogative   d) Declarative

5. I can't believe I lost my checkbook!

a) Exclamatory   b) Imperative

c) Interrogative   d) Declarative

6. Do you like Dairy Queen's burger or do you like Sonic's burger better?

a) Exclamatory   b) Imperative

c) Interrogative   d) Declarative

7. I ate the entire cake myself!

a) Exclamatory   b) Imperative

c) Interrogative   d) Declarative

8. Bring me two pencils and a black ink pen, please.

a) Exclamatory   b) Imperative

c) Interrogative d) Declarative

9. The astronaut opened the panel and drifted though it to the observation deck of the spacecraft.

a) Exclamatory b) Imperative

c) Interrogative d) Declarative

10. Are you planning on going to the county fair next week?

a) Exclamatory b) Imperative

c) Interrogative d) Declarative

11. When we go to Disneyland, we get to go on all the rides!

a) Exclamatory b) Imperative

c) Interrogative d) Declarative

12. John could neither find the puppy nor the red ball he had thrown for it to chase.

a) Exclamatory b) Imperative

c) Interrogative d) Declarative

13. Go back home and get the canoe so we can use it on the river.

a) Exclamatory b) Imperative

c) Interrogative d) Declarative

14. The puppy came running from the bushes for it had found the red ball.

a) Exclamatory b) Imperative

c) Interrogative d) Declarative

15. The fly flew into the room and landed on the boy's head.

a) Exclamatory b) Imperative

c) Interrogative d) Declarative

16. I cannot risk any more of my money gambling!

a) Exclamatory b) Imperative

c) Interrogative d) Declarative

17. The cowboy nor his friend knew how to fire the six shooter.

a) Exclamatory

b) Imperative

c) Interrogative

d) Declarative

18. There was a reason for the giant mural of the spaceman painted on the side of the building, but no one knew what it was.

a) Exclamatory

b) Imperative

c) Interrogative

d) Declarative

19. Do you want tacos for dinner, or do you want hamburgers?

a) do

b) you

c) or

d) want

20. Please make me some tacos.

a) Exclamatory

b) Imperative

c) Interrogative

d) Declarative

Chapter 13
Subjects and Predicates

13.0 Subjects and Predicates

A complete sentence requires three components: 1. a subject. 2. a predicate (verb) and 3. a complete thought.

Let us examine each of these components.

13.1 Subject

The subject is what or whom the sentence is about. It can be a noun, a pronoun, or a gerund (see chapter 16 for the definition of a gerund.) Usually, the subject comes before the verb (predicate.) The subject takes the verb in the sentence.

Single (simple) subject: John is my best friend. John is the subject because he is who the sentence is about.

The cave is dark and wet. Cave is the subject because the cave is what the sentence is about.

Compound subject: He and she are my friends. he and she are both subjects together joined by a coordinating conjunction. They are who the sentence is about. The sentence has a single verb which makes the sentence structure still a simple sentence.

Another example: Cars and trucks are both motor vehicles.

13.2 Predicate

Predicate: the predicate is the verb part of the sentence and often tells something about the subject. You can actually define the predicate as everything in the sentence except the subject.

Simple predicate: John cried. John is the subject and cried is the predicate.

Compound verb: Just like with a subject, a verb can be compound too. Jill walked to the table and picked up the glass. Walked and picked are both verbs. Jill did both things.

In chapter 18 we will talk more about predicates and verbs.

13.3 Complete Thought

The sentence needs to make sense. When we say a phrase or clause cannot stand on its own as a complete sentence, we are saying it does not complete a thought. "Around the corner" or "because Jill dropped the pizza" are not sentences because they are just sentence fragments and don't make sense alone.

Because jill dropped the pizza what? We need a main clause to complete it. Because Jill dropped the pizza, she had to buy another one. Now it makes sense.

We ran around the corner. Now the phrase "around the corner" makes sense too. We simply had to add the subject and the verb. "we ran"

Subject and Predicate Exercise

Directions: Underline the subject of each clause in the following sentences once and double underline the verb or verb phrases.

The thousand injuries of Fortunato I had borne as best I could; but when he ventured upon insult, I vowed revenge. You, who so well know the

nature of my soul, will not suppose, however, that I gave utterance to a threat. At length I would be avenged; this was a point definitively settled—but the very definitiveness with which it was resolved precluded the idea of risk. I must not only punish, but punish with impunity. A

wrong is unredressed when retribution overtakes its redresser. It is equally unredressed when the avenger fails to make himself felt as such to

him who has done the wrong.

13.4 Simple Subject and Complete Subject

The <u>simple subject</u> is one word that tells what a sentence is about.

EXAMPLE: My generous <u>father</u> makes certain I have plenty of money for school activities. <u>Father</u> is the simple subject.

The <u>complete subject</u> is all the words and phrases that describe (modify) the subject.

EXAMPLE: [My generous <u>father</u>] makes certain I have plenty of money for school activities. [My generous father] is the complete subject.

EXERCISES: Write the simple and complete subject of each sentence.

   1. The scared cat climbed up the tree.

Simple Subject: _____

Complete Subject: _____

2. My new, blue car got a flat tire.

Simple Subject: _____

Complete Subject: _____

3. My new winter coat keeps me warm in the winter.

Simple Subject: _____

Complete Subject: _____

4. The overworked delivery driver brought my package early.

Simple Subject: _____

Complete Subject: _____

5. A huge airplane flew over our house.

Simple Subject: _____

Complete Subject: _____

6. My Math class was canceled due to heavy snow in the area.

Simple Subject: _____

Complete Subject: _____

7. The hot sun was making the sand too hot to stand on for long.

Simple Subject: _____

Complete Subject: _____

8. The excited children arrived at the amusement park.

Simple Subject: _____

Complete Subject: _____

13.5 Simple Predicate and Complete Predicate

The simple predicate is the verb or verb phrase in a sentence.

EXAMPLE: The basketball team practiced in the newly built gymnasium. practiced is the simple predicate.

The complete predicate is all the words and phrases that describe (modify) the subject.

EXAMPLE: The basketball team [practiced in the newly built gymnasium]. [practiced in the newly built gymnasium.] is the complete predicate. In fact, the complete predicate can be defined as everything except the subject and it's modifiers.

EXERCISES: Write the simple and complete predicate of each sentence.

1. A new drive in opened in our area.

Simple Predicate: _____

Complete Predicate: _____

2. Mom bought many gifts online this year.

Simple Predicate: _____

Complete Predicate: _____

3. My cell phone screen cracked when I dropped it.

Simple Predicate: _____

Complete Predicate: _____

4. My aunt's house flooded during a storm last week.

Simple Predicate: _____

Complete Predicate: _____

5. I deleted old pictures from my cell phone.

Simple Predicate: _____

Complete Predicate: _____

6. Wind Turbines use wind to make electricity.

Simple Predicate: _____

Complete Predicate: _____

7. The students enjoyed their trip to the science fair.

Simple Predicate: _____

Complete Predicate: _____

8. People wash their hands to prevent diseases.

Simple Predicate: _____

Complete Predicate: _____

EXERCISES: Simple and Complete Subject and Predicate.

Directions: Write the simple and complete subject and predicate of each sentence.

1. Reusable shopping bags help to reduce plastic pollution.

Simple Subject: _____

Complete Subject: _____

Simple Predicate: _____

Complete Predicate: _____

2. My curious dog heard a noise in our backyard.

Simple Subject: _____

Complete Subject: _____

Simple Predicate: _____

Complete Predicate: _____

3. The strong and committed team won the championship.

Simple Subject: _____

Complete Subject: _____

Simple Predicate: _____

Complete Predicate: _____

4. The old and tired car still made the trip to the mountains.

Simple Subject: _____

Complete Subject: _____

Simple Predicate: _____

Complete Predicate: _____

Chapter 14
Transitive and Intransitive Verbs

14.0 Transitive and Intransitive Verbs

In English grammar, verbs can be classified as either transitive or intransitive based on their usage in a sentence. Understanding the difference between these two types of verbs is essential for constructing grammatically correct sentences because being able to identify them will help with identifying direct and indirect objects.

Transitive Verbs

A transitive verb is a verb that requires a direct object to complete its meaning. The direct object is the person, place, thing, concept, or idea that receives the action of the verb. For example:

She ate an apple. (The apple is receiving the action of the verb ate. It's being eaten.)

He wrote a letter. (The letter is receiving the action of the verb wrote. It's being written.)

In both of these examples, the action of the verb (eating and writing) is directed towards a specific object (an apple and a letter).

Intransitive Verbs

An intransitive verb is a verb that does not require a direct object to complete its meaning. These verbs usually describe an action or a state of being that does not involve a specific recipient of the action. For example:

She sneezed loudly. (Nothing is receiving the action of the sneeze. This verb is intransitive.)

He slept all day. (Nothing is receiving the action of the verb slept. This verb is intransitive)

In both of these examples, the verbs do not have a specific object that receives the action. Instead, they describe an action or state of being without involving a direct recipient.

This lesson is easy, right. You can always figure out if the verb is transitive or intransitive, right? What about this sentence:

Ivan drove to the store.

Is drove transitive or intransitive? It's intransitive because the store is the object of a preposition and not a direct object receiving the action of drove.

What about this sentence?

Sally wrote a love note for Jeff.

If you said wrote is transitive, you're right. "for Jeff" is a prepositional phrase, but note is the direct object and is receiving the action of being written.

Transitive and intransitive verbs are important concepts in English grammar, and understanding their differences is essential for constructing grammatically correct sentences. Transitive verbs require a direct object to complete their meaning, while intransitive verbs do not. Be careful not to mistake objects of the preposition for direct objects. (for more about direct objects see chapter 18)

Practice Exercises:

What is a transitive verb?

What is an intransitive verb?

How do you identify a transitive verb in a sentence?

How do you identify an intransitive verb in a sentence?

What is the difference between a direct object and an indirect object?

Can an intransitive verb have an object?

What is the role of a direct object in a sentence with a transitive verb?

What is the role of a subject in a sentence with an intransitive verb?

Can a verb be both transitive and intransitive?

How can you change a transitive verb into an intransitive verb?

Multiple Choice:

11. What is a transitive verb?

a) A verb that does not require an object

b) A verb that requires a direct object to complete its meaning

c) A verb that requires an indirect object to complete its meaning

12. What is an intransitive verb?

a) A verb that does not require an object

b) A verb that requires a direct object to complete its meaning

c) A verb that requires an indirect object to complete its meaning

13. Which of the following verbs is transitive?

a) Sleep

b) Run

c) Eat

14. Which of the following verbs is intransitive?

a) Hit

b) Laugh

c) Read

15. What is the role of a direct object in a sentence with a transitive verb?

a) It performs the action of the verb

b) It receives the action of the verb

c) It identifies the subject of the sentence

16. Can an intransitive verb have an object?

a) Yes, it always requires an object

b) No, it never requires an object

c) It depends on the context in which it is used

17. What is the role of a subject in a sentence with an intransitive verb?

a) It performs the action of the verb

b) It receives the action of the verb

c) It is the object of the verb

18. Can a verb be both transitive and intransitive?

a) Yes, depending on the context in which it is used

b) No, a verb can only be one or the other

c) It depends on whether it has a direct or indirect object

19. Which of the following sentences contains a transitive verb?

a) The sun rose early this morning.

b) The boy ran quickly to the store.

c) The teacher gave a quiz to the students.

20. How can you change a transitive verb into an intransitive verb?

a) By adding a direct object to the sentence

b) By removing the direct object from the sentence

c) By changing the verb tense

Transitive and Intransitive Verbs

Directions: Read each sentence. Determine if the action verb is being used as a Transitive or Intransitive verb. Circle your response.

1. Jason and Nicole cooked steaks in their back yard.

a)   Transitive   b)   Intransitive

2. Mrs. Jenny went to the grocery store, but she forgot to buy milk.

a)   Transitive   b)   Intransitive

3. Kelly knew she couldn't eat the entire cake.

a)   Transitive   b)   Intransitive

4. Steven drove his car way too fast on the interstate.

a)   Transitive   b)   Intransitive

5. Shawn was happy when she found her checkbook.

a)   Transitive   b)   Intransitive

6. Do you like Dairy Queen's burger or do you like Sonic's burger better?

a)   Transitive   b)   Intransitive

7. I love eating lemon cake.

a)   Transitive   b)   Intransitive

8. Jimmy rode into the sunset on his last day at the ranch.

a)   Transitive   b)   Intransitive

9. The astronaut on the ship looked at the stars outside his window.

a)   Transitive   b)   Intransitive

10.   The camp was pitched on the mountain on the other side of the range.

a) Transitive b) Intransitive

11. The superhero was afraid to get caught up in his cape, so he got rid of it.

a) Transitive b) Intransitive

12. John opened the jar for his mother.

a) Transitive b) Intransitive

13. John threw the red ball to his new puppy who ran after it happily.

a) Transitive b) Intransitive

14. The puppy came running from the bushes.

a) Transitive b) Intransitive

15. The fly flew into the room and landed on the boy's head.

a) Transitive b) Intransitive

16. I broke the sticks in half and threw them on the fire.

a) Transitive b) Intransitive

17. The cowboy cocked his pistol and prepared to fire it down the gun range.

a) Transitive b) Intransitive

18. There was a reason for the giant mural of the spaceman painted on the side of the building, but no one knew what it was.

a) Transitive b) Intransitive

19. Do you want tacos for dinner?

a) Transitive b) Intransitive

20. I wanted tacos so mother made them for me.

a) Transitive b) Intransitive

Chapter 15

The Five Sentence Structures

15.0 Five Sentence Structures:

15.1 Subject/Verb:

John cried.

John (subject) Cried (verb)

15.2 Subject/Verb/Direct Object:

Jason bought a car.

Jason (subject) bought (verb) a (article) car (direct object)

15.3 Subject/Verb/Complement:

Samantha is a very pretty woman.

Samantha (subject) is (linking verb) "a very pretty woman" is telling about the subject Samantha so it is the subject complement. A very pretty woman is being linked with "is" to Samantha, the subject.

15.4 Subject/Verb/Indirect Object/Direct Object:

Savanah sent John a letter.

Savanah is the subject, She is sending the letter (direct object.) The person she is she sending the letter to, is John, so John is the indirect object. "Letter" is taking the action of the verb "sent" and John is receiving the letter being sent. He is indirectly receiving the action of the verb.

15. 5 Subject/Verb/Direct Object/ Object Complement:

The presidential candidate thinks himself clever.

Like a subject complement, the word linked to the noun telling you something about that noun is the complement. In this case the object complement is telling us about the object of the sentence, "Himself" Himself is receiving the action of "thinks" Clever is telling you about the object "himself" so "himself" is the object complement.

<h1>Chapter 16</h1>

<h1>Predicate Nominatives and Predicate Adjectives</h1>

16.0 Predicate Adjectives and Predicate Nominatives

For verbs to be transitive they are usually action verbs, but what about verbs of being and linking verbs? Well, we have some ground to cover for verbs of being too. Predicate adjectives and predicate nominatives are two types of words that can be used in a sentence to describe the subject. In other words, these are adjectives or nouns that tell you something directly about the subject and are joined by linking verbs.

Predicate Adjectives

A predicate adjective is an adjective that follows a linking verb and tells something about the subject of the sentence. Linking verbs are verbs of being or verbs that have to do with the five senses, which can be action verbs or linking verbs. Linking verbs include "be," "seem," "appear," "taste," "look," and "become." For example:

The cake smells delicious.

(The linking verb is "smells," and "delicious" is the predicate adjective. You can tell "smells" is the linking verb and not an action verb because the subject "cake" is not doing the action of smelling. Don't let your desert smell you!)

She seems happy today.

(The linking verb is "seems," and "happy" is the predicate adjective. Seem is a vague verb but here it works. I would suggest you eliminate the verb "seem" in creative writing as much as possible. If it "seems" like a duck. It is indeed a duck! But, if you're not sure the person is actually happy like in the aforementioned sentence the verb "seem" works fine.)

In both of these examples, the predicate adjective follows a linking verb and describes the subject of the sentence (the cake and she, respectively).

Be careful: "That celebrity is a handsome man." Handsome is not a predicate adjective in this sentence because it's an adjective describing man and not celebrity. Man is the predicate nominative though.

Predicate Nominatives

A predicate nominative is a noun or pronoun that follows a linking verb and renames or identifies the subject of the sentence. You could also call it the predicate noun or pronoun if you are uncomfortable with nominative. "Nom" or "nominis" is Latin for "name". For example:

The winner of the race is John. (The "winner" is "John" John is the predicate nominative because "John" is renaming the "winner" which is the subject of the sentence.)

The new teacher is Mrs. Smith. (The "teacher" is "Mrs. Smith" Mrs. Smith is the predicate nominative because "Mrs. Smith" is renaming the "teacher" which is the subject of the sentence.)

In both of these examples, the predicate nominative follows a linking verb and renames or identifies the subject of the sentence (the winner and the new teacher, respectively).

Predicate adjectives and predicate nominatives are important components of English grammar. Predicate adjectives describe the subject of the sentence, while predicate nominatives rename or identify the subject of the sentence. Before you ask, yes, a sentence can have both a predicate adjective and predicate nominative.

Like this: Shirley is an engineer and is nice. Or Shirley is an engineer, and she is nice. Either way is fine. ("Engineer" is the P.N. and nice is the P.A.) Note: In the first sentence Shirley is both renamed and described. In the second sentence, which is a compound sentence, "Shirley" is renamed, and "she" is described. It's still one sentence but it has two clauses. See how useful knowing the difference between phrases and clauses can be!

Exercises:

1. Which of the following contains a predicate nominative?

a.) The bird flew high.

b.) The book is interesting.

c.) The cat meowed loudly.

d.) The girl ran fast.

2. Which of the following contains a predicate adjective?

a.) The sun is bright.

b.) The dog barked loudly.

c.) The car drove quickly.

d.) The tree grew tall.

3. In the sentence "She looks tired," what is the predicate adjective?

a.) looks

b.) tired

c.) She

d.) In

4. In the sentence "He seems nice," what is the predicate adjective?

a.) seems

b.) He

c.) nice

d.) In

5. In the sentence "The cake tasted delicious," what is the predicate adjective?

a.) tasted

b.) delicious

c.) The cake

d.) In

6. In the sentence "My brother became a doctor," what is the predicate nominative?

a.) became

b.) My brother

c.) doctor

d.) In

7. In the sentence "The flowers smell sweet," what is the predicate adjective?

a.) smell

b.) sweet

c.) The flowers

d.) In

8. In the sentence "The soup is hot," what is the predicate adjective?

a.) is

b.) hot

c.) The soup

d.) In

9. In the sentence "The movie seemed boring," what is the predicate adjective?

a.) seemed

b.) boring

c.) The movie

d.) In

10. In the sentence "They appeared nervous," what is the predicate adjective?

a.) appeared

b.) nervous

c.) They

d.) In

Predicate Nominatives & Predicate Adjectives

Part 1 Predicate Nominatives

Directions: Read each sentence. Determine which one of your answer choices is being used as a Predicate Nominative. Circle your response.

1. Jill is the golf player whom I am coaching.

a) golf
b) whom
c) Jill
d) player

2. You have been a loyal friend to me!

a) have
b) loyal
c) friend
d) to

3. Sabastian is the only baritone auditioning for the role.

a) role
b) auditioning
c) only
d) baritone

4. Arachnophobia is the fear of insects with eight legs like spiders and scorpions.

a) arachnophobia
b) insects
c) fear
d) eight

5. Are you and Tate good friends?

a) friends
b) tate
c) good
d) you

6. Is French one of the Romance languages?

a) French
b) languages
c) Romance
d) one

7. Have you always been an avid fan of pro football?

a) avid
b) fan
c) football
d) you

8. Everyone in that performance school is an excellent dancer.

a) everyone   b) excellent

c) dancer   d) performance

9. Two members of the bowling team are Jack and Jill.

a) members   b) bowling

c) team   d) Jack, Jill

10. Was he the one who fell from the stage?

a) one   b) stage

c) he   d) who

Part 2 Predicate Adjectives

Directions: Read each sentence. Determine which one of your answer choices is being used as a Predicate Adjective. Circle your response.

11. This song was popular during the winter of 2005.

a) song   b) winter

c) popular   d) during

12. Does that burrito taste too spicy?

a) does   b) spicy

c) burrito   d) too

13. Are these sheep free to roam the range?

a) sheep   b) range

c) these   d) free

14. My sister is three years older than I am.

a) my   b) sister

c) older   d) I

15. All winter the weather here has been cold and wet.

a) all   b) weather

c) winter   d) cold, wet

16. Why does this cheese always smell so pungent?

a) cheese   b) why

c) smell   d) pungent

17. The blueberries will be ripe in a few days.

a) ripe   b) blueberries

c) days   d) will

18. This fruit is not only delicious but also good for you.

a) good   b) but

c) delicious   d) you

19. The stadium audience grew restless waiting for the batter to swing.

a) audience   b) restless

c) waiting   d) batter

20. The actor portraying Henry V in the play was wrong for the part.

a) actor   b) play

c) part   d) wrong

Chapter 17
Direct and Indirect Objects

17.0 Direct/Indirect Objects

Direct and indirect objects are two types of objects that can be used in a sentence to receive the action of the verb. Objects can be either nouns, pronouns, or even gerunds.

Direct Objects

A direct object is a noun or pronoun that directly receives the action of the verb. The direct object answers the question "What?" or "Whom?" after the verb. For example:

He kicked the ball. (The verb is "kicked," and "the ball" is the direct object. Kicked is transitive.)

She ate the sandwich. (The verb is "ate," and "the sandwich" is the direct object. Ate is transitive.)

In both of these examples, the direct object receives the action of the verb (kicked and ate).

Indirect Objects

An indirect object is a noun or pronoun that receives the direct object. The indirect object answers the question "To whom?" or "For whom?" after the verb. For example:

He gave the ball to his friend.

(The verb is "gave," "the ball" is the direct object, and "his friend" is the indirect object.) Because "friend" is the object of a preposition, it might be easier to see the indirect object if the sentence were written like this instead: **He gave his friend the ball.**

The ball was given. To whom was the ball given? (His friend.) Friend is the indirect object.

She bought a present for her sister.

(The verb is "bought," "a present" is the direct object, and "her sister" is the indirect object.) **She bought her sister a present.** The present was bought. For whom was the present bought? (Her sister) Sister is the indirect object.

In both of these examples, the indirect object receives the direct object (the ball and the present).

Direct and indirect objects are important components of English grammar. Direct objects receive the action of the verb, while indirect objects receive the direct object. If you can identify the direct object and then ask "to whom?" or "for whom?" and there is an answer in the sentence, that is the indirect object.

Pre-Quiz Practice Exercises:

1. What is the direct object in the following sentence: "The dog chased the cat"?

a) dog

b) cat

c) chased

2. Which of the following sentences has an indirect object?

a) She bought a new car.

b) He gave the book to her.

c) They played soccer in the park.

3. What is the indirect object in the sentence: "The teacher gave the students a quiz"?

a) teacher

b) quiz

c) students

4. In the sentence "I wrote my mom a letter," what is the direct object?

a) wrote

b) mom

c) letter

5. What is the indirect object in the sentence: "She told me a secret"?

a) secret

b) me

c) told

6. Which of the following sentences has a direct object?

a) She danced all night.

b) He talked to his friend on the phone.

c) They went to the movies together.

7. What is the indirect object in the sentence: "He baked his mom a cake"?

a) mom

b) cake

c) baked

8. In the sentence "The doctor prescribed medication for her," what is the direct object?

a) prescribed

b) doctor

c) medication

9. What is the direct object in the sentence: "They watched a movie at the theater"?

a) watched

b) movie

c) theater

10. Which of the following sentences has both a direct and indirect object?

a) She read the book in one sitting.

b) He gave his sister a gift for her birthday.

c) They walked to the store and back.

Direct Objects and Indirect Objects

Directions: Read each sentence. Determine which one of your answer choices is being used as a Direct Object. Circle your response.

Part 1 Direct Objects

1. Jason and Nicole found a box of coins buried in their back yard.

a) a
b) found
c) coins
d) box

2. Mrs. Jenny bought bread when she went shopping yesterday.

a) buy
b) the
c) bread
d) to

3. Kelly knew she couldn't eat the entire cake, yet she tried to eat it all anyway.

a) knew
b) all
c) to
d) cake

4. Steven drove his car onto the freeway.

a) car
b) the
c) freeway
d) onto

5. Shawn couldn't find her checkbook.

a) find
b) her
c) couldn't
d) checkbook

6. Do you like Dairy Queen's hamburgers?

a) Dairy Queen
b) do
c) like
d) hamburgers

7. I love lemon cake, so I ate half of it myself.

a) it
b) lemon
c) cake
d) so

8. Mrs. Johnson didn't want to go to the movies, but she did anyway.

a) anyway
b) didn't

c) no direct object   d) movies

9. The astronaut opened the panel and drifted though it to the observation deck of the spacecraft.

a) of   b) panel

c) the   d) It

10. The principal wanted to cancel the game due to snow, yet he knew how important it was for the game to continue.

a) game   b) it

c) yet   d) was

Part 2 Indirect Objects

Directions: Read each sentence. Determine which one of your answer choices is being used as an Indirect Object. Circle your response.

11. Jill sent her boyfriend John a letter telling him about her week.

a) boyfriend   b) John

c) letter   d) her

12. Ron gave his son Jack a puppy for his birthday.

a) birthday   b) his

c) Jack   d) son

13. He bought the puppy a new collar at the general store.

a) he   b) puppy

c) the   d) collar

14. Jack threw the puppy a red ball to play with.

a) puppy   b) To play

c) threw   d) ball

15. The witness gave the policeman a detailed report on the incident.

a) witness   b) policeman

c) report   d) incident

16. Mr. Dutton bought his wife a car for her birthday.

a) for

b) car

c) wife

d) his

17. The bride told the groom the bad news.

a) groom

b) the

c) news

d) bad

18. The science professor assigned the class two homework projects.

a) projects

b) class

c) assigned

d) professor

19. Do you like to read your children a story before putting them to bed?

a) story

b) read

c) before

d) children

20. The butler brought his employer warm milk to help with sleep.

a) brought

b) sleep

c) butler

d) employer

Chapter 18
Subject and Object Complements

18.0 Subject and Object Complements

Remember predicate adjectives and predicate nominatives? It turns out when you have something in the predicate telling you something about the subject, we have a name for that. It's called a complement. You can have a subject complement, or an object complement. (Compliment with an "I" would be like "You look nice today." Complement with an "E" means it goes together. It's complimentary. Like "That dress goes with your figure. The dress complements your figure.

Subject Complements

A subject complement is a word or phrase that follows a linking verb and describes or renames the subject of the sentence. Sound familiar? Subject complements can be either predicate adjectives or predicate nominatives, which were covered in Chapter 17. For example:

My favorite color is blue. (The linking verb is "is," and "blue" is the predicate nominative that renames "my favorite color." Blue is the subject complement.)

She seems tired. (The linking verb is "seems," and "tired" is the predicate adjective that describes "she." Tired is the subject complement.)

In both of these examples, the subject complement follows a linking verb and describes or renames the subject of the sentence. Now on to newer territory.

Object Complements

An object complement is a word or phrase that follows a direct object and completes its meaning. Object complements can be either predicate adjectives or predicate nominatives. For example:

They painted the wall blue. (The direct object is "the wall," and "blue" is the object complement that describes it.)

The teacher considered him a genius. (The direct object is "him," and "a genius" is the object complement that renames him.)

In both of these examples, the object complement follows the direct object and completes its meaning.

This chapter probably could have been included in chapter 17, but I thought I would give you more practice with predicate nominative and predicate adjectives!

Practice Exercises:

1. What is the subject complement in the sentence: "The cake smells delicious"?

a) cake

b) smells

c) delicious

2. Which of the following sentences has an object complement?

a) She ate a sandwich for lunch.

b) He painted the walls blue.

c) They went to the beach on vacation.

3. What is the object complement in the sentence: "She considered him her best friend"?

a) considered

b) friend

c) him

4. In the sentence "The teacher called her students intelligent," what is the subject complement?

a) called

b) teacher

c) intelligent

5. What is the object complement in the sentence: "He made his daughter a birthday cake"?

a) made

b) daughter

c) cake

6. Which of the following sentences has a subject complement?

a) She walked to the store.

b) He bought a new car.

c) They felt happy after the party.

7. What is the object complement in the sentence: "I consider traveling a learning experience"?

a) consider

b) traveling

c) experience

8. In the sentence "The doctor declared her healthy," what is the subject complement?

a) declared

b) doctor

c) healthy

9. What is the subject complement in the sentence: "The flowers looked beautiful in the sunlight"?

a) looked

b) flowers

c) beautiful

10. Which of the following sentences has both a subject and object complement?

a) She found the movie boring.

b) He gave his mom a bouquet of flowers.

c) They listened to music on the radio.

Chapter 19
Verbals

19.0 Verbals

Now, if you are happy with a basic grammar knowledge and you have reached this point, you are ready for some more advanced English grammar lessons. Advanced English grammar lessons begin now.

Verbals are words that look like verbs, but they function as different parts of speech in a sentence. It's like some verbs don't want to be verbs and instead want to be something else. There are three types of verbals: gerunds, participles, and infinitives. In this chapter, we will define each type of verbal, provide examples of how to use them correctly, and explain their roles in a sentence.

Gerunds

I have mentioned gerunds before. These are important to understand.

A gerund is a verbal that always ends in -ing and functions as a noun in a sentence, but it cannot be preceded by a helping verb. It can be the subject of a sentence, the object of a verb, or the object of a preposition. For example:

<u>Swimming</u> is good exercise. (subject of the sentence)

She loves <u>reading</u> books. (object of the verb "loves")

I am not good at <u>cooking</u>. (object of the preposition "at")

But not Jared is cooking us dinner. Because cooking has the helping verb is, it is actually a verb phrase "is cooking" and not a gerund.

If you ever take a test and see this question, you will understand why it's important to know what a gerund is:

Question: Which one of these words is a verb in this sentence. Choose all that apply.

Lying, stealing, and cheating are wrong.

> 1. lying
>
> 2. stealing
>
> 3. cheating
>
> 4. are
>
> 5. all of the above.

You might choose all of the above because they all look like verbs, but the answer is d) are. The others are all gerunds. In fact, lying, stealing, and cheating are the subjects of the sentence.

Participles

Participles are verbals that can function as adjectives in a sentence. In other words, they look like verbs but modify a noun like an adjective. There are two types of participles: present participles (-ing) and past participles (-ed or irregular). For example:

The <u>running</u> water is refreshing. (present participle as an adjective) running modifies/describes water.

The <u>broken</u> vase needs to be replaced. (past participle as an adjective) broken modifies/describes vase.

Don't dangle your participles.

Filled with deep potholes, the school bus driver drove down the road. This dangling participle makes it seem as if the school bus driver is filled with deep potholes instead of the road. Make the deep potholes point to the road not the driver. The school bus driver drove down a road filled with deep potholes.

Infinitives

An infinitive is a verbal formed by adding "to" before the base form of a verb (e.g., to eat, to run). It can function as a noun, an adjective, or an adverb in a sentence, but it's obviously not the main verb. For example:

To dance is my favorite hobby. (subject of the sentence)

She has a lot of work to do. (adjective modifying "work")

He stayed up late to finish his project. (adverb modifying "stayed up")

Split Infinitive:

My beloved Star Trek's opening monologue contains a split infinitive! To boldly go where no one has gone before. "To boldly go" is a split infinitive. It should be read "to go boldly" where no one has gone before. You are not supposed to put an adverb or anything between the infinitive "to" and its verb. If you do, you have a split infinitive. This used to be a big deal back in the olden days, but it's not that big of a thing anymore. Nowadays, I regularly see split infinitives in mainstream books.

Verbal Practice Exercises:

1. Which of the following is NOT a type of verbal?

a) Infinitive

b) Gerund

c) Participle

d) Conjunction

2. What is the function of a gerund in a sentence?

a) To act as a verb

b) To act as an adjective

c) To act as an adverb

d) To act as a noun

3. Which of the following sentences contains a participle?

a) The boy who is running is fast.

b) Running is good exercise.

c) I am excited to see the movie.

d) The teacher handed out the graded papers.

4. In the sentence "I want to swim in the pool," what part of speech is "to swim"?

a) Gerund

b) Infinitive

c) Present participle

d) Past participle

5. Which of the following sentences contains a gerund phrase?

a) The book sitting on the table is mine.

b) She likes to read books in her free time.

c) Running shoes are essential for exercise.

d) The painting, created by a famous artist, sold for millions.

6. In the sentence "The bird flying overhead was a bald eagle," what part of speech is "flying"?

a) Gerund

b) Infinitive

c) Present participle

d) Past participle

7. Which of the following sentences contains an infinitive phrase?

a) He told a joke that was not funny.

b) The girl singing the solo has a beautiful voice.

c) To run a marathon, you need to train hard.

d) I am tired of listening to your excuses.

8. In the sentence "The dog, wagging its tail, ran to the door," what part of speech is "wagging"?

a) Gerund

b) Infinitive

c) Present participle

d) Past participle

9. Which of the following sentences contains a participial phrase?

a) She likes to ride her bike on the weekends.

b) The old man, walking slowly, crossed the street.

c) To write a good essay, you need to have a clear thesis statement.

d) The children were playing in the park.

10. What is the difference between a participle and a gerund?

a) A participle acts as a verb, while a gerund acts as an adjective or adverb.

b) A participle always ends in -ing, while a gerund can end in -ing or -ed.

c) A participle acts as an adjective or adverb, while a gerund acts as a noun.

d) A participle is used in the present tense, while a gerund is used in the past tense.

Chapter 20
Determiners

20.0 Determiners

Determiners are words used in front of a noun to make it clear as to whom or what the noun refers to.

20.1 The 4 types of Determiners

Articles both definite and indefinite.

Articles are "the," "a," and "an."

Indefinite articles introduce a general version of the noun: **An** elephant never forgets**.** or **A** cat would be **a** great pet for you.

The definite article "the" introduces a specific noun. **The** car is a Rolls Royce. or **We have the** best BBQ in **the** state.

Possessives

Possessives show ownership and include "ours," "yours," "hers," "his," "mine," and "theirs."
Introduces a noun that belongs or is owned by someone.

The place on the left is **my** house.

Which house is **your** house?

Quantifiers

Quantifiers are the words "all," "few," and "many."

Indicates how much or how little of the noun there is: He has a **few** new cars on the lot.

There was not **much** food left when we arrived at the party.

Demonstrative

These point to a specific noun. That include "that," "there," "these. " "this," and "those."

Who do **these** children belong to?

I am unable to ride **this** horse.

Determiner Exercises

Directions: Choose the determiner that best fits in the blank.

1. I have _____ pencils on the shelf but I don't have _____ erasers.

2. At twelve o'clock we had_____ food.

3. My father bought _____ amazing car.

4. Are you coming to _____ party next Saturday?

5. Look at ___ the deer crossing the road.

6. Would you like to come over to _____house?

7. There are _____ jobs you can do without a college degree.

8. I need_____men to help me clear the field.

9. Look at all _____ books.

10. We don't need _____ administrators telling us what to teach in class.

Chapter 21

Punctuation and Mechanics

21.0 Punctuation and Mechanics

Finally, punctuation and mechanics are the finishing touches that give a sentence its polish and clarity. In this final basic grammar chapter, we'll explore the different types of punctuation, their functions, and the rules for using them correctly. We'll also discuss common errors and offer strategies for avoiding them.

Punctuation and mechanics are essential components of English grammar. They help us to convey meaning and clarify our writing. Consider "Let's eat grandma." Without the correct punctuation it seems this person is wanting to devour their grandma for dinner! "Let's eat, grandma." Tells the reader the person is beckoning for grandma to come have a meal.

21.1 Capitalization

Capitalization refers to the use of capital letters at the beginning of sentences, proper nouns, and the first letter of important words in titles. It is important to use capitalization correctly, as it can affect the meaning of a sentence. For example:

Incorrect: i went to the piggly wiggly.

Correct: I went to the Piggly Wiggly.

21.2 Punctuation Marks

Period (.) - The period is used to indicate the end of a sentence. It's sometimes called a full stop.

Question Mark (?) - The question mark is used to indicate a direct question.

Exclamation Mark (!) - The exclamation mark is used to indicate strong emotion or emphasis. One will suffice. Writing fourteen of them in a row really isn't necessary.

Comma (,) - The comma is used to separate items in a list, to separate clauses in a sentence, and to clarify meaning. Probably the most abused and wrongly used punctuation mark. I have tried to teach its usage throughout this book. The oxford comma is one of the main controversial topics in English grammar. The oxford comma is the comma right before the conjunction in a series: I like apples, bananas, (the oxford comma) and oranges. I was taught when I was in school in the 1980s to leave it out. But, as an adult with an editor, I have been told to put it in! I personally say what does it hurt to just go ahead and include it? No one will count it wrong if you do, but they might count it wrong if you don't.

Semi-colon (;) - The semi-colon is used to separate two related independent clauses in a sentence. It is also used in a series where commas already exist. For example: I have visited Oklahoma City, Oklahoma; Austin, Texas; Kansas City, Kansas and New York, New York.

Colon (:) - The colon is used to introduce a list, a quote, or a summary. You can use it correctly be saying. I have a list of Halloween candies (and here they are) in place where the semicolon goes.

Apostrophe (') - The apostrophe is used to indicate possession or contraction.

Quotation Marks (" ") - Quotation marks are used to indicate a direct quote or to indicate that a word is being used in a specific sense. They are essential in creative writing to indicate dialogue.

21.3 Mechanics

Mechanics refer to the technical aspects of writing, such as spelling, grammar, and formatting. Mechanics are important but you need not worry about them until you are in the editing phase of your work.

Spelling - Correct spelling is important for clear communication. Spelling errors can change the meaning of a sentence and may cause confusion. The English language is full of homophones and homographs. I once used maul in place of maw when referring to a dragon. The first one, Maul is a hammer, the second is the mouth and snout of the dragon.

Grammar - Correct grammar is essential for clear and effective communication. Grammatical errors can change the meaning of a sentence and may affect the reader's understanding. This is where knowing the parts of speech and how they work comes into play. If you understand the parts of speech, you understand grammar.

Formatting - Correct formatting is important for clear and effective communication. This includes the use of margins, spacing, and font size. When writing an essay for example, one should not use frilly fonts or font sizes that are too big. This is why many English teachers give you the formatting instructions for a paper before you are assigned to write it.

Exercises:

1. What is the purpose of a comma?

a) To indicate a pause in speech

b) To separate items in a list

c) Both a and b

2. Which of the following is not a type of sentence ending punctuation?

a) Period

b) Comma

c) Exclamation point

3. When should a semicolon be used?

a) To separate items in a list

b) To join two independent clauses without a conjunction

c) To indicate a pause in speech

4. Which of the following is a correct way to use a colon?

a) Before a list

b) After a verb

c) Between a subject and a predicate

5. What is the purpose of quotation marks?

a) To indicate a pause in speech

b) To show a direct quote

c) To separate items in a list

6. Which of the following is not a type of dash?

a) En dash

b) Em dash

c) Hyphen

7. What is the purpose of an ellipsis?

a) To indicate a pause in speech

b) To show omission of words in a quote

c) To separate items in a list

8. What is the purpose of parentheses?

a) To show emphasis

b) To enclose additional information

c) Both a and b

9. What is the purpose of a hyphen?

a) To indicate a pause in speech

b) To connect two words

c) Both a and b

10. Which of the following is a correct way to use an apostrophe?

a) To form contractions

b) To show possession

c) Both a and b

11. Which of the following is a correct way to use capitalization?

a) To capitalize the first letter of every word in a sentence

b) To capitalize proper nouns and the first word of a sentence

c) To capitalize only the first word of a sentence

12. Which of the following is a correct way to use a question mark?

a) To end a declarative sentence

b) To end an interrogative sentence

c) To indicate excitement or emphasis

13. What is the purpose of a slash?

a) To indicate a pause in speech

b) To indicate a choice between two options

c) To separate items in a list

14. Which of the following is a correct way to use a bullet point?

a) To separate items in a list

b) To indicate emphasis

c) To show a quote

15. Which of the following is a correct way to use an exclamation point?

a) To end a declarative sentence

b) To end an interrogative sentence

c) To indicate excitement or emphasis

Cumulative Quiz 2: Grammar and Mechanics

Directions: Read each sentence. Determine which one of your answer choices is being used as a coordinating conjunction. Circle your response.

Identify the Sentence Structure

1. I wish you would help me clean the house more, but I know you're tired when you get home from work.

   a) declarative   b) imperative

   c) interrogative   d) exclamatory

2. How can you be as old as you are and be so lazy at the same time?

   a) declarative   b) imperative

   c) interrogative   d) exclamatory

3. Bring me the wrench from the green toolbox.

   a) declarative   b) imperative

   c) interrogative   d) exclamatory

Identify the verb as Transitive or Intransitive

4. I wrote a letter to the editor.

   a) transitive   b) intransitive

   c) wrote   d) not an action verb

5. There is a good reason to clean the house every day.

   a) transitive   b) intransitive

   c) is   d) not an action verb

6. Are you going to the dance this afternoon?

   a) transitive   b) intransitive

   c) are going   d) not an action verb

Identify the Predicate Nominative

7. Barbara is an engineer and she's very pretty.

   a) engineer   b) pretty

Cumulative Quiz 2 Answers

1. A
2. C
3. B
4. A
5. D
6. B
7. A
8. B
9. C
10. D
11. C
12. C
13. B
14. B
15. A
16. D
17. A
18. C
19. A
20. B
21. B
22. C
23. A
24. D
25. C
26. A
27. A
28. A
29. C
30. A
31. A
32. D
33. B
34. D

a) ring

b) each

c) his

d) daughters

17. She wrote him a nice letter.

a) him

b) wrote

c) letter

d) nice

18. He gave the player a free throw.

a) free

b) throw

c) player

d) he

Identify whether the sentence is written in Active or Passive voice.

19. She was given a present.

a) passive

b) active

20. He gave her a nice gift and then they left for the movies.

a) passive

b) active

21. John wanted to go.

a) passive

b) active

Identify the Gerund.

22. I am really not good at lying.

a) really

b) am

c) lying

d) good

23. Loading the car for the trip is not easy.

a) loading

b) car

c) trip

d) is

24. Hoarding, storing, and keeping materials from others is wrong.

a) hoarding

b) storing

c) keeping	d) <u>all of the above</u>

Identify the Participle or Participial phrase.

25. I sat beside a babbling brook.

a) sat	b) brook
c) babbling	d) I

26. Filled with deep potholes, the road was desperately in need of repairs.

a) filled with deep potholes	b) desperately in need
c) filled	d) of repairs

27. The handyman was hired to fix the shattered tiles in the bathroom.

a) shattered	b) hired
c) handyman	d) in the bathroom

Identify the Infinitve or Infinitive phrase.

28. I like to run in marathons.

a) to run	b) both a and d
c) like	d) in marathons

29. My job is to water the lawn and to care for the flowers.

a) to water	b) to care
c) both a & b	d) no infinitive

30. I want you to be the new spokesman.

a) to be	b) new
c) want	d) no infinitive

Identify the Sentence Type

31. Jason and Jack ran as fast as they could to the neighbor's house.

a) simple	b) compound
c) complex	d) compound-complex

32. Jessica went shopping at the mall, but she didn't buy anything because she left her wallet at home.

a) simple	b) compound

c) complex

d) compound-complex.

33. Fred Johnson is the new janitor; he will be here later today.

a) simple

b) compound

c) complex

d) compound-complex.

Indicate the correct mood in which the following sentences are written.

34. You will wash the car today.

a) simple

b) subjective

c) imperative

d) indicative

35. I wish I were a rich man.

a) simple

b) subjective

c) imperative

d) indicative

36. Find out what the new employee's name is for me.

a) simple

b) subjective

c) imperative

d) indicative

37. If you were to fight in the ring, you would be annihilated!

a) simple

b) subjective

c) imperative

d) indicative

38. You will need to stop by the grocery store on the way home from school today.

a) simple

b) subjective

c) imperative

d) indicative

39. Stop making all that noise, please!

a) simple

b) subjective

c) imperative

d) indicative

40. You can wish you were a doctor all you want but you're not one.

a) simple

b) subjective

c) imperative

d) indicative

Chapter 22

Indicative, Imperative, and Subjunctive Mood

22.0 Indicative, Imperative, and Subjunctive Mood

English has three verb moods which indicates the speaker's attitude towards what is being said.

The three verb form moods include indicative, imperative, and subjunctive.

The Indicative Mood

The Indicative mood is for stating facts and opinions.

Examples: I am going to discuss your attitude with you.

You will clean your room today!

I love listening to the band The Warning.

All the above sentences state a fact. Indicative moon can also deny a fact.

You do not know how to clean properly.

The president will not attend the meeting.

The Imperative Mood

The imperative mood is for giving orders and instructions. The following examples illustrate the different kinds of imperatives one can give. A

period indicates a mild command while an exclamation point indicates a strong command.

Look out! (you) look out (issuing a warning)

Leave the building now! (you) leave the building now. (giving an order)

Please form a line at the front of the room. (you) please form a a line at the front of the room. (making a request)

Follow the arrows on the floor and then turn left at the double doors. (you) follow the arrows on the floor and then turn left at the double doors. (giving instructions)

The Subjunctive Mood

The subjunctive mood is a verb form that expresses various states of unreality such as wishes, hypothetical situations, or doubts. Subjunctive mood helps you to be able to easily tell if you should use "was" or "were" in a sentence. Once you understand subjunctive mood, you will never use "was" when you should have used "were" and vice versa again.

The subjunctive mood is used to express hypothetical or unlikely situations, unreal conditions, wishes, doubts, or commands. It is often used in the context of an "if" or "wish" clause or to express uncertainty, possibility, or necessity. The subjunctive mood is formed differently depending on the verb tense, but it usually involves changing the form of the verb.

Here are some examples of the subjunctive mood in use:

If I **were** rich, I would travel the world. (The verb "were" is in the subjunctive mood, expressing an unreal situation. If it's wishful thinking use "**were**")

I wish I **were** a rich man. (If and wish are good indications you should use the verb were.

I **was** a rich man. (If it's a statement of fact use was instead.)

It is important that she be here on time. (The verb "be" is in the subjunctive mood, expressing necessity or obligation.)

I suggest that he go to the doctor. (The verb "go" is in the subjunctive mood, expressing a suggestion or recommendation.)

Differences between Subjunctive and Indicative Moods

The subjunctive mood differs from the indicative mood in that it expresses states of unreality, while the indicative mood expresses facts, actions, and events that are true or certain. For example:

If it rains, I will stay inside. (The verb "rains" is in the indicative mood, expressing a fact or likelihood.) Rain is forecasted or is possible.

I **was** a rich man. (The verb "was" is in the indicative mood, expressing a fact. Were would indicate he was not a rich man.)

I wish I **were** a rich man. (wishful thinking and not a fact.)

If it were to rain, I would stay inside. (The verb "were" is in the subjunctive mood, expressing an unreal or hypothetical situation.) Rain is hypothetical. It may rain, it may not, no one has predicted it one way or the other.

Just remember to use "were" after "if" and "wish" if you are writing a sentence of wishful thinking, and use "was" when writing a sentence of fact and you will be fine. This will help in creative writing especially because it will help you discern between "were" and "was" more easily in most situations.

Mood Pre-Quiz Practice Exercises:

1. Which of the following sentences is in the indicative mood?

A) I wish I could go to the concert.

B) Go to the store and buy some milk.

C) If I were you, I would take the job.

D) Let's go to the beach this weekend.

2. Which of the following sentences is in the imperative mood?

A) He asked if she wanted to go for a walk.

B) Don't forget to turn off the lights.

C) I wonder what time the movie starts.

D) If only I had more free time.

3. Which of the following sentences is in the subjunctive mood?

A) She runs five miles every day.

B) If I had a million dollars, I would buy a mansion.

C) I am going to the store.

D) He always plays the guitar after dinner.

4. Which of the following sentences is in the indicative mood?

A) I hope the weather is nice tomorrow.

B) Be careful not to spill the coffee.

C) If I were taller, I would play basketball.

D) Let's have pizza for dinner tonight.

5. Which of the following sentences is in the imperative mood?

A) I wonder what he will say.

B) Don't be late for your appointment.

C) If only I had studied more for the test.

D) She always reads a book before going to bed.

6. Which of the following sentences is in the subjunctive mood?

A) They are running in the park.

B) If he were here, he would help us.

C) I will call you later.

D) Let's go to the zoo this weekend.

7. Which of the following sentences is in the indicative mood?

A) It's important that you arrive on time.

B) Make sure you bring a jacket.

C) If only I had taken that job offer.

D) Let's practice our dance routine again.

8. Which of the following sentences is in the imperative mood?

A) I wonder what the score will be.

B) Don't forget to lock the door.

C) If only I had more money.

D) She always wears a hat when it's sunny.

9. Which of the following sentences is in the subjunctive mood?

A) We are planning a trip to Hawaii.

B) If she were here, she would know what to do.

C) I am going to the gym after work.

D) Let's watch a movie tonight.

10. Which of the following sentences is in the indicative mood?

A) It's great that you got the job.

B) Take out the garbage before you go.

C) If only I could travel the world.

D) Let's go for a walk in the park.

11. Which of the following sentences is in the imperative mood?

A) I wonder what the chef will prepare.

B) Don't touch the hot stove.

C) If only I had more time to read.

D) He always goes for a run in the morning.

12. Which of the following sentences is in the subjunctive mood?

A) She is studying for her exam.

B) If we had more supplies, we could finish the project.

C) I am meeting my friend for lunch.

D) Let's go to the beach this weekend.

Chapter 23
Active and Passive Voice

23.0 Active and Passive Voice

Active and passive voice are two different ways of expressing the same idea in a sentence. Ah, the dreaded passive voice. Almost all creative writing advice tells you to avoid passive voice and always write in active voice, but is active voice always better in all situations?

Active Voice

In an active sentence, the subject of the sentence performs the action. Unless the sentence is inverted the subject is usually located at the beginning of the sentence, followed by a verb and an object. For example:

The cat chased the mouse. (The subject "cat" is actively chasing the object "mouse.")

In an active sentence, the subject is doing the action, which makes the sentence more direct and clearer.

Passive Voice

In a passive sentence, the object of the sentence becomes the subject, and the verb is changed to a form of "be" followed by the past participle of the verb. (The past participle form of the verb is the verb you use with helping verbs like have, has, or had. Like this: I go skiing a lot, I went skiing last week, I have gone skiing on many occasions. "Gone" is the past participle form of the verb "go.") For example:

The mouse was chased by the cat. (The object "mouse" becomes the subject, and the verb "chased" is changed to "was chased" to form the past participle form of the verb "chase" and therefore formed the passive sentence.)

In a passive sentence, the subject is receiving the action, which makes the sentence less direct and less clear. Passive voice is often used to shift the focus away from the person performing the action and onto the action itself.

Here are some more examples of active and passive voice:

Active voice: The chef cooked the meal.

Passive voice: The meal was cooked by the chef.

In the active sentence, the subject "chef" performs the action of cooking. In the passive sentence, the object "meal" becomes the subject, and the verb "cooked" is changed to "was cooked" to form the passive sentence.

Active voice: The car ran the red light.

Passive Voice: The red light was run by the car.

Starting to see the pattern yet? Let's look at another:

Active voice: The company hired a new employee.

Passive voice: A new employee was hired by the company.

In the active sentence, the subject "company" performs the action of hiring. In the passive sentence, the object "new employee" becomes the subject, and the verb "hired" is changed to "was hired" to form the passive sentence.

Sometimes you just have to use was and passive voice. You should never eliminate all passive voice, but you should have a small percentage compared to active voice when you edit. Probably no more than 5% of your entire essay, manuscript, or story. If your scene is set at a funeral, it would be silly to write:

What a good friend was he, or What a good friend is he, or He is a good friend, when referring to the deceased. It would be: He was a good friend.

Consider:

Person 1: How did he die? Person 2: Friendly fire killed him. (Active)

Person 1: How did he die? Person 2: He was killed by friendly fire. (Passive)

It may be discouraged but sometimes it just looks, sounds, and reads better to use it anyway. But as you can see from the last example, it's also a matter of choice and opinion. Use passive voice sparingly and you will be fine.

Exercises:

1. Which of the following sentences is in active voice?

a) The cake was baked by my mom.

b) My mom baked the cake.

2. What is the passive voice form of the sentence "The teacher gave the students a test"?

a) The students were given a test by the teacher.

b) The teacher was giving the students a test.

3. In which of the following sentences is the subject in passive voice?

a) The cat chased the mouse.

b) The mouse was chased by the cat.

4. Which of the following sentences is in active voice?

a) The book was read by me.

b) I read the book.

5. What is the passive voice form of the sentence "They built a new house last year"?

a) A new house was built by them last year.

b) They were building a new house last year.

6. In which of the following sentences is the subject in passive voice?

a) The dog bit the mailman.

b) The mailman was bitten by the dog.

7. Which of the following sentences is in active voice?

a) The movie was watched by us.

b) We watched the movie.

8. What is the passive voice form of the sentence "She made a delicious cake"?

a) A delicious cake was made by her.

b) She was making a delicious cake.

9. In which of the following sentences is the subject in passive voice?

a) The teacher is teaching the lesson.

b) The lesson is being taught by the teacher.

10. Which of the following sentences is in active voice?

a) The song was sung by the choir.

b) The choir sang the song.

11. What is the passive voice form of the sentence "She wrote a book about her travels"?

a) A book about her travels was written by her.

b) She was writing a book about her travels.

12. In which of the following sentences is the subject in passive voice?

a) The baby is drinking the milk.

b) The milk is being drunk by the baby.

13. Which of the following sentences is in active voice?

a) The letter was written by my sister.

b) My sister wrote the letter.

14. What is the passive voice form of the sentence "He caught the ball"?

a) The ball was caught by him.

b) He was catching the ball.

15. In which of the following sentences is the subject in passive voice?

a) The chef is cooking the meal.

b) The meal is being cooked by the chef.

Part 3

Answer Keys

Chapter 24

Answers Keys to Exercises

Chapter 1 Nouns Exercises Answer Key:

1. A common noun is a noun that refers to a general or non-specific person, place, thing, or idea, such as "dog," "chair," or "idea."

2. A proper noun is a specific name of a person, place, or thing, such as "John," "Paris," or "Nike."

3. An abstract noun is a noun that refers to an intangible concept or idea, such as "love," "happiness," or "justice."

4. A concrete noun is a noun that refers to a tangible object or physical thing, such as "table," "tree," or "car."

5. A collective noun is a noun that refers to a group of people, animals, or things, such as "family," "herd," or "team."

6. A countable noun is a noun that can be counted and has a singular and plural form, such as "book" and "books."

7. A non-countable noun is a noun that cannot be counted and only has a singular form, such as "water," "money," or "advice."

8. A compound noun is a noun made up of two or more words that function as a single unit, such as "toothbrush," "laptop," or "sunflower."

9. A possessive noun is a noun that shows ownership or possession, such

as "John's car" or "the company's profits."

10. A singular noun is a noun that refers to one person, place, thing, or idea, such as "book," "chair," or "idea."

11. A plural noun is a noun that refers to more than one person, place, thing, or idea, such as "books," "chairs," or "ideas."

12. A denominal adjective is an adjective derived from a noun such as **school** bus or **tennis** player. Usually, by itself, the word is a noun. Also denominal adjectives are made by using proper nouns with a suffix like Dickensian or Reaganesque to describe a certain time or place.

Chapter 2 Verbs Exercises Answer key:

1. Answer: b

2. Answer: c

3. Answer: c

4. Answer: a

5. Answer: a

6. Answer: a

7. Answer: c

8. Answer: c

9. Answer: a

10. Answer: c

Chapter 3 Pronouns Exercises Answer keys:

1. Answer: c

2. Answer: c

3. Answer: d

4. Answer: a

5. Answer: d

6. Answer: d

7. Answer: d

8. Answer: a

9. Answer: b

10. Answer: c

11. Answer: a

12. Answer: a

13. Answer: c

14. Answer: c

15. Answer: a

Pronoun case and perspective Answers:

1.Answer: The subjective (nominative) case of pronouns is used as the subject of a sentence. Examples include: I, you, he, she, it, we, they.

2. Answer: The objective case of pronouns is used as the object of a verb or preposition. Examples include: me, you, him, her, it, us, them.

3. Answer: The possessive case of pronouns shows ownership or possession. Examples include: my, your, his, hers, its, our, their.

4. Answer: First-person perspective uses pronouns like "I" and "we" to refer to oneself or oneself and others. Second-person perspective uses pronouns like "you" to refer to the person being spoken to. Third-person perspective uses pronouns like "he," "she," and "they" to refer to someone or something that is not the speaker or the person being spoken to.

5. Answer: You should determine the appropriate pronoun case and perspective by identifying the role of the pronoun in the sentence (subject, object, possessive), and by considering the perspective from which the sentence is being written (first-person, second-person, third-person). Additionally, it is important to consider the context of the sentence and the intended meaning.

Chapter 4 Adjective Exercises Answer key:

Adjectives Answer Key

Part I: Underline the correct word(s) in the parentheses.

1. In ancient Roman times, salt was once (<u>more valued</u>, most valued) than silver.

2. It is (good, <u>better</u>) to ask a person for help than to receive it.

3. Our new boss is (more kind, <u>kinder</u>) than the last.

4. The (little, <u>less</u>) time I spend playing my guitar, the more guilty I feel.

Part II: Underline the adjective that modifies the bolded noun in each sentence.

1. The <u>kind</u> grandma made cookies.

2. The <u>quick</u> rabbit hopped across the road.

3. The <u>little</u> boy sang the song beautifully.

4. Those <u>red flashing</u> sirens are annoying.

5. An <u>old</u> dog barked at the moon.

Part III: Underline the group of words in the parentheses that show the adjective(s) in

their correct order.

1. The (<u>very quick bunny</u>, quick very bunny) hopped across the road.

2. At the bar, Jodi sang a/an (American classic, <u>classic American</u>) song for Karaoke Night.

3. The incessant noise of the police siren is very (<u>annoying</u>, annoyed).

4. The long day of teaching left Jill feeling (exhausting, <u>exhausted</u>).

5. Crazy Feather wore a (leather black jacket, <u>black leather jacket</u>) to the ceremonial dance

Chapter 5 Adverbs Exercises Answer key:

1. The bird sang **cheerfully**. Adverb Kind <u>   manner   </u>

2. What is your father doing **outside**? Adverb Kind <u> place </u>

3. John practices guitar four times **every day**. Adverb Kind <u> time </u>

4. We will let you know about the job **soon**. Adverb Kind <u>   time   </u>

5. The turtle crawled **slowly**. Adverb Kind <u> manner </u>

6. The ghosts are haunting **there**. Adverb Kind <u>   place   </u>

7. The machine **usually** comes on **automatically**. Adverb Kind <u> manner </u>

8. The woman took her bow **gracefully**. Adverb Kind <u> manner </u>

9. he bugs were flying **everywhere**. Adverb Kind <u> place </u>

Chapter 4-5: Adjective and Adverbs Exercises Answer Key:

1. Answer: b red

2. Answer: b well

3. Answer: b green

4. Answer: b quickly

5. Answer: b ugly

6. Answer: b easily

7. Answer: b brow

8. Answer: b carefully

9. Answer: b old

10. Answer: b slowly

11. Answer: b friendly

12. Answer: a beautiful

13. Answer: a hard

14. Answer: d easily

15. Answer: b hot

16. Answer: b honestly

17. Answer: b new

18. Answer: b quickly

19. Answer: b cold

20. Answer: d well

Chapter 6: Interjections Exercises Answer Key:

1. **b**

2. **b**

3. **c**

4. **b**

5. **b**

6. **b**

7. **b**

8. **b**

9. **b**

10. **b**

11. **b**

12. **a**

13. **b**

14. **a**

15. **b**

Chapter 7 Articles Exercises Answer Key:

1. d

2. b

3. c

4. a

5. c

6. d

7. b

8. b

9. b

10. c

11. c

12. b

13. c

14. b

15. b

Chapter 8 Phrases and Clauses Exercises Answer Key:

1. Answer: b

2. Answer: b

3. Answer: a

4. Answer: b

5. Answer: c

6. Answer: b

7. Answer: a

8. Answer: a

9. Answer: b

10. Answer: b

Chapter 8 Noun Phrases Exercises Answer Key:

1. A noun phrase is a group of words that includes a noun and any modifiers that describe or identify it.

2. The function of a noun phrase in a sentence is to act as the subject, object, or complement of a verb, or to serve as a modifier of another noun or noun phrase.

3. An appositive phrase in a noun phrase is a noun or noun phrase that renames or explains another noun or noun phrase in the sentence.

4. A relative clause in a noun phrase is a clause that begins with a relative pronoun and describes or identifies the noun or pronoun in the noun phrase.

5. A post-modifier in a noun phrase is a word or phrase that comes after the head noun and provides additional information about it.

6. A pre-modifier in a noun phrase is a word or phrase that comes before the head noun and provides additional information about it.

7. A noun clause in a noun phrase is a clause that functions as a noun and is introduced by a subordinating conjunction.

8. A complement in a noun phrase is a word or phrase that follows the head noun and provides additional information about it, such as an adjective or a noun clause.

9. A head noun in a noun phrase is the main noun that the phrase is

referring to and all other modifiers and phrases in the noun phrase are describing or identifying it.

Chapter 8: Adjective and Adverb Phrases Exercises Answer Key:

1. Answer: b A group of words that modify a noun or pronoun

2. Answer: b A group of words that modify a verb, adjective, or another adverb

3. Answer: b The car with the broken window

4. Answer: c The dog barked loudly

5. Answer: b To modify a noun or pronoun

6. Answer: b To modify a verb, adjective, or another adverb

7. Answer: a Yes

8. Answer: a Yes

9. Answer: b An adjective phrase modifies a noun or pronoun, while an adverb phrase modifies a verb, adjective, or another adverb.

10. Answer: b No

11. Answer: b No

12. Answer: a Yes

13. Answer: a Yes

14. Answer: a Yes

15. Answer: a Yes

Chapter 9: Prepositions Exercises Answer Key:

1. **Prepositions:**

1.Answer: A

2. Answer: C

3. Answer: B

4. Answer: C

5. Answer: C

6. Answer: A

7. Answer: B

8. Answer: A

9. Answer: A

10. Answer: A

Prepositions and Antecedents:

1.Answer: B

2. Answer: C

3. Answer: A

4. Answer: D

5. Answer: D

6. Answer: C

7. Answer: D

8. Answer: D

9. Answer: B

Chapter 10: Conjunctions Exercises Answer Key:

Coordinating Conjunctions:

1.Answer: c) and

2. Answer: b) but

3. Answer: c) or

4. Answer: d) for

5. Answer: d) so

6. Answer: d) if

7. Answer: a) and

8. Answer: d) as

9. Answer: d) yet

10. Answer: d) for

Subordinating Conjunctions:

1.Answer: B

2. Answer: B

3. Answer: C

4. Answer: A

5. Answer: C

6. Answer: B

7. Answer: C

8. Answer: B

9. Answer: A

10. Answer: D

Correlative Conjunctions:

1.Answer: C

2. Answer: C

3. Answer: D

4. Answer: A

5. Answer: D

Chapter 11: The Twelve Verb Tenses Exercises Answer Key:

1. Answer: b Future Simple

2. Answer: c Present Perfect Continuous

3. Answer: c Past Simple

4. Answer: b Past Simple

5. Answer: b Future Continuous

6. Answer: b Past Perfect

7. Answer: b Present Continuous

8. Answer: c Future Perfect

9. Answer: b Past Perfect

10. Answer: b Future Perfect Continuous

11. Answer: a Future Simple

12. Answer: a Past Simple

13. Answer: c Past Continuous

14. Answer: a Past Perfect

15. Answer: b Future Simple

Chapter 12: Sentence Types Exercises Answer Key:

1. Answer: a

2. Answer: c

3. Answer: a

4. Answer: d

5. Answer: b

6. Answer: b

7. Answer: c

8. Answer: a

9. Answer: d

10. Answer: d

11. Answer: c

12. Answer: d

13. Answer: a

14. Answer: a

15. Answer: b

Chapter 12: Sentence Structure Exercises Answer Key:

1. Answer: b

2. Answer: c

3. Answer: a

4. Answer: a

5. Answer: b

6. Answer: a

7. Answer: a

8. Answer: b

9. Answer: a

10. Answer: a

Chapter 13: Subjects and Verbs Exercises Answer Key:

Subjects are **bolded** and Verbs/Verb Phrases are italicized

The thousand **injuries** of Fortunato I had borne as best I could; but when **he** ventured upon insult, **I** vowed revenge. **You**, who so well know the

nature of my soul, will not suppose, however, that **I** gave utterance to a threat. At length **I** would be avenged; **this** was a point definitively

settled—but the very definitiveness with which **it** was resolved precluded the idea of risk. **I** must not only punish, but punish with impunity. A

wrong is unredressed when retribution overtakes its redresser. **It** is equally unredressed when the **avenger** fails to make himself felt as such to

him who has done the wrong.

Chapter 14: Transitive and Intransitive Verbs Exercises Answer Key:

1. A transitive verb is a verb that requires a direct object to complete its meaning.

2. An intransitive verb is a verb that does not require a direct object to complete its meaning.

3. A transitive verb can be identified by looking for a verb that has a direct object following it in the sentence.

4. An intransitive verb can be identified by looking for a verb that does not have a direct object following it in the sentence.

5. A direct object is a noun or pronoun that receives the action of a transitive verb, while an indirect object is a noun or pronoun that receives the direct object of the transitive verb.

6. No, an intransitive verb cannot have an object.

7. The direct object in a sentence with a transitive verb receives the action of the verb and answers the question "what?" or "whom?"

8. The subject in a sentence with an intransitive verb performs the action of the verb and answers the question "who?" or "what?"

9. Yes, some verbs can be both transitive and intransitive, depending on the context in which they are used.

10. To change a transitive verb into an intransitive verb, you can remove the direct object from the sentence.

Multiple Choice:

1. Answer: b

2. Answer: a

3. Answer: c

4. Answer: b

5. Answer: b

6. Answer: b

7. Answer: a

8. Answer: a

9. Answer: c

10. Answer: b

Chapter 16: Predicate Adjectives and Predicate Nominatives Exercises Answer Key:

1. Answer: b. The book is interesting.

2. Answer: a. The sun is bright.

3. Answer: b. tired

4. Answer: c. nice

5. Answer: b. delicious

6. Answer: c. doctor

7. Answer: b. sweet

8. Answer: b. hot

9. Answer: b. boring

10. Answer: b. nervous

Chapter 17: Direct and Indirect Objects Exercises Answer Key:

1. Answer: b cat

2. Answer: b He gave the book to her.

3. Answer: c students

4. Answer: c letter

5. Answer: b me

6. Answer: b He talked to his friend on the phone.

7. Answer: a mom

8. Answer: c medication

9. Answer: b movie

10. Answer: b He gave his sister a gift for her birthday.

Chapter 18: Subject and Object Complements Exercises Answer Key:

1. Answer: c delicious

2. Answer: b He painted the walls blue.

3. Answer: b friend

4. Answer: c intelligent

5. Answer: c cake

6. Answer: c They felt happy after the party.

7. Answer: b traveling

8. Answer: c healthy

9. Answer: c beautiful

10. Answer: a She found the movie boring.

Chapter 19: Verbals Exercises Answer Key:

1. Answer: d Conjunction

2. Answer: d To act as a noun

3. Answer: a The boy who is running is fast.

4. Answer: b Infinitive

5. Answer: c Running shoes are essential for exercise.

6. Answer: c Present participle

7. Answer: c To run a marathon, you need to train hard.

8. Answer: c Present participle

9. Answer: b The old man, walking slowly, crossed the street.

10. Answer: c A participle acts as an adjective or adverb, while a gerund acts as a noun.

Chapter 20: Determiners Exercises Answer Key:

Directions: Choose the determiner that best fits in the blank.

1. I have <u>some</u> pencils on the shelf but I don't have **any** erasers.

2. At twelve o'clock we had **some** food.

3. My father bought **an** amazing car.

4. Are you coming to **the** party next Saturday?

5. Look at **all** the deer crossing the road.

6. Would you like to come over to **the** house?

7. There are **many** jobs you can do without a college degree.

8. I need **some** men to help me clear the field.

9. Look at all **those** books.

10. We don't need **any** administrators telling us what to teach in class.

Chapter 21: Punctuation and Mechanics Exercises Answer Key:

1. Answer: c

2. Answer: b

3. Answer: b

4. Answer: a

5. Answer: b

6. Answer: c

7. Answer: b

8. Answer: c

9. Answer: b

10. Answer: c

11. Answer: b

12. Answer: b

13. Answer: b

14. Answer: a

15. Answer: c

Chapter 22: Indicative, Imperative, and Subjunctive Mood Exercises Answer Key:

1. Answer: a

2. Answer: b

3. Answer: b

4. Answer: a

5. Answer: b

6. Answer: b

7. Answer: a

8. Answer: b

9. Answer: b

10. Answer: b

11. Answer: b

12. Answer: b

Chapter 23: Active and Passive Voice Exercises Answer Key:

1. Answer: b My mom baked the cake.

2. Answer: a The students were given a test by the teacher.

3. Answer: b The mouse was chased by the cat.

4. Answer: b I read the book.

5. Answer: b The mailman was bitten by the dog.

6. Answer: b We watched the movie.

7. Answer: a A delicious cake was made by her.

8. Answer: b The lesson is being taught by the teacher.

9. Answer: b The choir sang the song.

10. Answer: a A book about her travels was written by her.

11. Answer: b The milk is being drunk by the baby.

12. Answer: b My sister wrote the letter.

13. Answer: a The ball was caught by him.

14. Answer: b The meal is being cooked by the chef.

Noun Worksheet Answers

1. A
2. A
3. C
4. A
5. B
6. D
7. C
8. D
9. A
10. B
11. D
12. C
13. B
14. C
15. A
16. A
17. C
18. D
19. C
20. B
21. C
22. C
23. D
24. B
25. A
26. B
27. D
28. C
29. D
30. C

Verbs, Infinitives, Gerunds

Answer Key

1. **C**
2. **A**
3. **D**
4. **C**
5. **B**
6. **A**
7. **B**
8. **D**
9. **C**
10. **B**
11. **A**
12. **C**
13. **A**
14. **D**
15. **B**
16. **C**
17. **B**
18. **D**
19. **B**
20. **C**
21. **D**
22. **A**
23. **A**
24. **C**
25. **D**
26. **C**
27. **D**
28. **D**
29. **B**
30. **A**

Pronouns and Antecedents

Answer Key

1. **C**
2. **A**
3. **B**
4. **D**
5. **B**
6. **D**
7. **C**
8. **A**
9. **B**
10. **A**
11. **D**
12. **C**
13. **B**
14. **A**
15. **B**
16. **D**
17. **C**
18. **D**
19. **A**
20. **B**

Adjective or Adverb?

1. **C**
2. **B**
3. **D**
4. **D**
5. **C**
6. **A**
7. **C**
8. **B**
9. **B**
10. **A**
11. **D**
12. **A**
13. **C**
14. **D**
15. **B**

Interjections Worksheet

Answer Key

1. **A**
2. **B**
3. **D**
4. **C**
5. **A**
6. **B**
7. **B**
8. **B**
9. **B**
10. **C**
11. **C**
12. **A**
13. **C**
14. **C**
15. **D**
16. **B**
17. **D**
18. **B**
19. **C**
20. **B**

Articles Worksheet

Answer Key

1. **A**
2. **C**
3. **D**
4. **B**
5. **C**
6. **A**
7. **D**
8. **D**
9. **B**
10. **C**
11. **A**
12. **A**
13. **D**
14. **B**
15. **C**
16. **A**
17. **D**
18. **B**
19. **C**
20. **B**

Prepositions Worksheet
Answer Key

1. **D**
2. **A**
3. **B**
4. **D**
5. **B**
6. **A**
7. **D**
8. **D**
9. **B**
10. **A**
11. **C**
12. **D**
13. **A**
14. **D**
15. **B**
16. **C**
17. **C**
18. **D**

19. **A**
20. **B**
21. **D**
22. **C**
23. **A**
24. **C**
25. **D**
26. **B**
27. **D**
28. **C**
29. **C**
30. **B**

Coordinating Conjunctions Answer Key

1. **D**
2. **C**
3. **D**
4. **B**
5. **C**
6. **A**
7. **D**
8. **D**
9. **B**
10. **C**
11. **C**
12. **A**
13. **D**
14. **B**
15. **C**
16. **A**
17. **D**
18. **B**
19. **C**
20. **B**

Subordinating Conjunctions
Worksheet Answers

1. **A**
2. **D**
3. **C**
4. **B**
5. **C**
6. **A**
7. **D**
8. **B**
9. **B**
10. **C**
11. **D**
12. **B**
13. **C**
14. **D**
15. **C**
16. **B**
17. **A**
18. **C**
19. **D**
20. **D**

Sentence Types Worksheet

Answer Key

1. **D**
2. **D**
3. **D**
4. **C**
5. **A**
6. **C**
7. **A**
8. **B**
9. **D**
10. **C**
11. **C**
12. **D**
13. **B**
14. **D**
15. **D**
16. **A**
17. **D**
18. **C**
19. **D**
20. **B**

Subject and Predicate Paragraph Answer Key

The simple subject is underlined and the simple predicate is italicized.

The thousand injuries of Fortunato I had borne as best I could; but when he ventured upon insult, I vowed revenge. You, who so well know the

nature of my soul, will not suppose, however, that I gave utterance to a threat. At length I would be avenged; this was a point definitively

settled—but the very definitiveness with which it was resolved precluded the idea of risk. I must not only punish, but punish with impunity. A

wrong is unredressed when retribution overtakes its redresser. It is equally unredressed when the avenger fails to make himself felt as such to

him who has done the wrong.

Simple and Complete Subjects and Predicates Exercises Answer keys

EXERCISES: Write the simple and complete subject of each sentence.

1. The scared cat climbed up the tree.

Simple Subject: _____cat_____

Complete Subject: _____the scared cat_____

2. My new, blue car got a flat tire.

Simple Subject: _____car_____

Complete Subject: _____My new, blue car_____

3. My new winter coat keeps me warm in the winter.

Simple Subject: _____coat_____

Complete Subject: _____My new winter coat_____

4. The overworked delivery driver brought my package early.

Simple Subject: _____driver_____

Complete Subject: ___The overworked delivery driver_____

5. A huge airplane flew over our house.

Simple Subject: _____airplane_____

Complete Subject: _____A huge airplane_____

6. My Math class was canceled due to heavy snow in the area.

Simple Subject: _____class_____

Complete Subject: _____My Math class_____

7. The hot sun was making the sand too hot to stand on for long.

Simple Subject: _____sun_____

Complete Subject: _____The hot sun_____

8. The excited children arrived at the amusement park.

Simple Subject: _____children_____

Complete Subject: _____The excited children_____

EXERCISES: Write the simple and complete predicate of each sentence.

    1. A new drive in opened in our area.

Simple Predicate: _____opened_____

Complete Predicate: ____opened in our area_____

2. Mom bought many gifts online this year.

Simple Predicate: _____bought_____

Complete Predicate: _bought many gifts online this year____

3. My cell phone screen cracked when I dropped it.

Simple Predicate: ____cracked_____

Complete Predicate: _____cracked when I dropped it_____

4. My aunt's house flooded during a storm last week.

Simple Predicate: _____flooded_____

Complete Predicate: __flooded during a storm last week___

5. I deleted old pictures from my cell phone.

Simple Predicate: _____deleted_____

Complete Predicate: __deleted old pictures from my cell phone_

6. Wind Turbines use wind to make electricity.

Simple Predicate: _____use_____

Complete Predicate: __use wind to make electricity_____

7. The students enjoyed their trip to the science fair.

Simple Predicate: _____enjoyed_____

Complete Predicate: __enjoyed their trip to the science fair___

8. People wash their hands to prevent diseases.

Simple Predicate: _____wash_____

Complete Predicate: __wash their hands to prevent diseases___

EXERCISES: Simple and Complete Subject and Predicate.

Directions: Write the simple and complete subject and predicate of each sentence.

    1. Reusable shopping bags help to reduce plastic pollution.

Simple Subject: _____bags_____

Complete Subject: __Reusable shopping bags_____

Simple Predicate: ___help_____

Complete Predicate: ___help to reduce plastic pollution_____

2. My curious dog heard a noise in our backyard.

Simple Subject: ____dog_____

Complete Subject: <u>My curious dog</u>

Simple Predicate: <u>heard</u>

Complete Predicate: <u>heard a noise in our backyard</u>

3. The strong and committed team won the championship.

Simple Subject: <u>team</u>

Complete Subject: <u>The strong and committed team</u>

Simple Predicate: <u>won</u>

Complete Predicate: <u>won the championship</u>

4. The old and tired car still made the trip to the mountains.

Simple Subject: <u>car</u>

Complete Subject: <u>The old and tired car</u>

Simple Predicate: <u>made</u>

Complete Predicate: <u>made the trip to the mountains</u>

Transitive and Intransitive Verbs Worksheet

Answer Key

1. **A**
2. **B**
3. **A**
4. **A**
5. **A**
6. **A**
7. **A**
8. **B**
9. **B**
10. **B**
11. **B**
12. **A**
13. **A**
14. **B**
15. **B**
16. **A**
17. **A**
18. **B**
19. **A**
20. **A**

Predicate Nominatives and Predicate Adjectives Worksheet

Answer Key

1. D
2. **C**
3. **D**
4. **C**
5. **A**
6. **D**
7. **B**
8. **C**
9. **D**
10. **A**
11. **C**
12. **B**
13. **D**
14. **C**
15. **D**
16. **D**
17. **A**
18. **C**
19. **B**
20. **D**

Direct Objects and Indirect Objects Worksheet
Answer Key

1. **D**
2. **C**
3. **D**
4. **A**
5. **D**
6. **D**
7. **C**
8. **C**
9. **B**
10. **A**
11. **B**
12. **C**
13. **B**
14. **A**
15. **B**
16. **C**
17. **C**
18. **B**
19. **D**
20. **D**

Cumulative Quiz 1 Answers

1. A
2. C
3. D
4. B
5. C
6. A
7. B
8. C
9. D
10. C
11. C
12. A
13. D
14. B
15. A
16. C
17. A
18. D
19. D
20. B
21. A
22. B
23. A
24. D
25. A
26. C
27. B
28. A
29. C
30. A
31. A
32. C
33. B
34. D

35. C
36. B
37. C
38. D
39. B
40. C

Cumulative Quiz 2 Answers

1. A
2. C
3. B
4. A
5. D
6. B
7. A
8. B
9. C
10. D
11. C
12. C
13. B
14. B
15. A
16. D
17. A
18. C
19. A
20. B
21. B
22. C
23. A
24. D
25. C
26. A
27. A
28. A
29. C
30. A
31. A
32. D
33. B
34. D

35. B
36. C
37. B
38. D
39. C
40. B

Made in United States
Troutdale, OR
11/30/2024

25413304R00151